What Every Church Member Should Know About Poverty

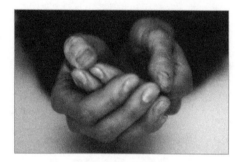

What Every Church Member Should Know About Poverty

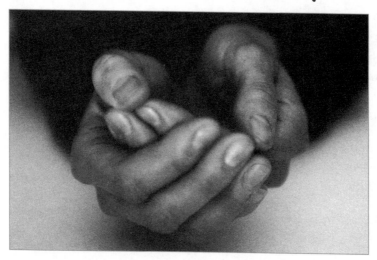

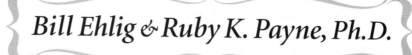

Bill Ehlig & Ruby K. Payne, Ph.D.

aha!
Process, Inc.

aha! Process, Inc.
P.O. Box 727
Highlands, TX 77562-0727
(800) 424-9484 ■ (281) 426-5300
Fax: (281) 426-5600
Website: www.ahaprocess.com

Printed in the United States of America
Book design by Sara Patton
Copy editing by Dan Shenk

Ehlig, Bill, & Payne, Ruby K.
    What Every Church Member Should Know About Poverty
    152 pp.
    Bibliography pp. 133–136
    ISBN-13: 978-1-929229-50-5
    ISBN-10: 1-929229-50-X
    1. Education   2. Sociology   3. Title

CONTENTS

FOREWORD

As churches engage in urban ministries and invite the poor into their congregations, many issues arise. This book attempts to address some of the issues that churches face in dealing with individuals from poverty. The book also is intended to continue the conversation about how your congregation can better serve the poor.

Each chapter has a scenario/story about an incident. An explanation of the issues involved in the scenario follows. Most chapters conclude with some observations and questions for the congregation to consider.

Since churches are largely about relationships and beliefs, it is important that this information be tailored and discussed in terms of your particular congregation, as well as your denomination and its doctrinal heritage. This book is not meant to provide answers. It is rather a source of information that can be used to assist with your decision making.

The Christian church began in the cities. Although Jesus spent much (but not all) of his ministry in villages, the primary work of the apostles was in places like Jerusalem, Caesarea, Antioch, Athens, Corinth, and Rome. Eventually, Christianity spread from what were often cosmopolitan centers to more remote areas. The word "pagan" witnesses to this later development. Pagan means "one from the country."

In the United States it has been only since World War II and the new dominance of city population that churches have faced many of the current issues of urban life. This is especially true in the South. Unemployment, homelessness, and huge economic gulfs had little or no part in the rural setting of many of our grandparents. Many Christians are befuddled by the challenges of the city. There are obvious difficulties in the loneliness possible in a crowd. The anonymity of huge populations can bring a darkness of its own. But Christians are called to be light. So have we been, and so may we yet be.

PREFACE TO SECOND EDITION

In the late 1990s Dr. Ruby K. Payne and I decided to take the ideas within *A Framework for Understanding Poverty* and apply them to the church setting. The exploration of life resources, language registers, and hidden rules had already helped middle-class schoolteachers as they worked with families in poverty. The application of these ideas to churches and Christian organizations also has been useful—as revealed in workshops and special studies the past six years in which this book has been a focal point.

This second edition of "The Church Book" is a continuation of the effort. We have added another chapter (a new Chapter 12) describing the use of a "Resources Inventory" to better understand existing and/or needed resources among those serving and being served. We also have updated the economic and demographic data in the back of the book; cultural and linguistic shifts of recent decades have presented complicated challenges to churches in the United States.

Individuals are encouraged to read *What Every Church Member Should Know About Poverty* on their own, but many church groups also find it helpful to use the book as a study tool. There are two basic approaches I would recommend for interested groups:

- The standard 13-week quarterly. The book has 13 chapters, so it is ideally suited to the traditional Sunday school study format.

- A five-week course for mid-week groups or Sunday school classes that want to give attention to this issue but not over a long period of time. I recommend five thematically grouped units of about 25 pages each, as follows:

The Biblical mandate is clear; both the Old Testament and the New Testament have literally hundreds of admonitions to respond in love to the needs of the poor. May our responses to need around and among us flow out of the compassion of Jesus himself.

– Bill Ehlig

What Every Church Member Should Know About Poverty

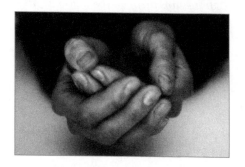

SCRIPTURES/ECCLESIASTICUS

Happy are those who consider the poor; the LORD delivers them in the day of trouble. The LORD protects them and keeps them alive; they are called happy in the land. You do not give them up to the will of their enemies. The LORD sustains them on their sickbed; in their illness you heal all their infirmities.

— Psalm 41:1–3

If you close your ear to the cry of the poor, you will cry out and not be heard.

— Proverbs 21:13

My child, do not cheat the poor of their living, and do not keep needy eyes waiting. Do not grieve the hungry, or anger one in need. Do not add to the troubles of the desperate, or delay giving to the needy. Do not reject a suppliant in distress, or turn your face away from the poor. Do not avert your eye from the needy, and give no one reason to curse you; for if in bitterness of soul some should curse you, their Creator will hear their prayer.

— Ecclesiasticus 4:1–6

CHAPTER 1

Introduction and Overview

A Story

In the ancient story, a man sat by the city dump. Though once blessed in many ways, he had about lost it all: his health, his wealth, and his children. Such a person was, in the eyes of that age, destitute. Health gave hope for the day's labor. Wealth was power to face the bigger trials. Children would mean protection and someone to lean upon in the closing years. All were now gone.

The situation was difficult for him to comprehend. Nothing in his experience had prepared him for such catastrophes. He had followed the rules. He had been an exemplary, even notable, citizen. In his mind he wondered at the extent of the disaster. He could not find a reason for it. As he sat in the pain of his crumbling body, he doubted he could keep his sanity.

Along came three of his friends who had known him in the blessed times. They too sat down in consternation. Only in their case the difficulty was not pain or hopelessness, rather it was how to make sense of such troubles. They concluded: "God must be angry at you because of your sins for you to suffer so." And that's just what they told him.

From ages ago we have this story of the troubles of Job. His three friends came to him and offered thoughts that were comforting, that is, comforting to themselves. It is easier to deal with the problems of others in need if you decide that their troubles have been caused by their own willful sin. In that case, you can take part in the "justice" of the situation when you do not help at all. Should you choose to help, even just a little, such magnanimity would show your great virtue.

In the eyes of Eliphaz, Bildad, and Zophar, Job had caused his own suffering. But at the conclusion of the Book of Job, their counsel was condemned by God Himself. As the world has done since the time of Job, we struggle today with the phenomenon of people in need, sometimes great need. Is it sufficient for God's people to offer no more than the foolish counsel of Job's friends?

Part, at least, of their folly was a failure to see deeply enough into Job's situation. The purpose of this book is to help individuals to look deeper, even into themselves, as well as into the lives of those who have need.

Some key points about poverty need to be made.

1. Poverty and wealth are relative. We basically know our own poverty or wealth only in relationship to others.

2. Poverty occurs in all races and countries. The notion of middle class as a large segment of society is a phenomenon of the past 100 years. In the United States the largest group of individuals in poverty is children under the age of 18. If one counts the number of children in poverty or very close to it, the number is close to 50%. One of the biggest misconceptions is the difference between percentages and numbers. The greatest number of children in poverty are white, but the greatest percentage of children in poverty is by minority group.

3. Generational and situational poverty are different. It generally takes two generations to make the transition from middle class into poverty. When an individual has been in poverty two generations or more, then the patterns and habits are different. Situational poverty is when there is a divorce, death, or illness,

and the resources are temporarily reduced, but the mindset remains largely with middle-class norms and values.

4. This work is based upon patterns of the group, and all patterns have exceptions.

5. Every individual brings with him or her the hidden rules of the economic group in which he or she was raised. Hidden rules are those unspoken cueing mechanisms we use to let people know they do or do not belong.

6. Schools and businesses use the hidden rules of middle class. So do many churches. Because America now tends to be economically segregated, most individuals do not know the rules of other economic classes.

7. For churches to be successful with the poor, members must understand the hidden rules of generational poverty, as well as middle class, so that the transition can be more readily accepted. For the transition to occur, both sets of rules must be openly acknowledged.

8. To move from poverty to middle-class norms and values, a period of time exists where some relationships are broken. These relationships may be resumed at another time, but there is a period of time in which the old relationships are very tentative and, sometimes, broken.

9. The fundamental reasons for poverty are lack of educational attainment and the disconnection of family and/or community.

10. Four reasons one leaves poverty: It's too painful to stay, a vision or goal, a key relationship, or a special talent or skill.

OBSERVATION

A soul must have certain resources to keep life going on a given day or week—resources like air, water, food, a sufficient distance from sharp objects. To look forward more than a few days takes another list of resources—things like knowledge, friends, health, a sense of purpose or hope, and wisdom. Lacking a significant amount of these is not only life-threatening, it is also fairly obvious. It is obvious to those around who do not want to contract whatever disease troubles the deprived soul or who do not wish to waste their limited resources upon one who may not survive anyway. What am I to do when presented with one who is short on survival resources? It is an old problem, and one with which the Bible grappled long ago.

QUESTIONS

1. What would your parents/grandparents think of your current possessions?

2. If your grandparents could return at your age now, how would they relate to your friends and their interests?

3. What rules for the use of money did you develop from your experiences in life?

4. What places can you visit and feel at home? Why?

5. Where have you been and felt completely foreign?

6. A group project: Spend 30 minutes or an hour trying to determine what it costs to live an independent life in your community. Include basic housing, home maintenance (utilities, appliances, furniture, etc.), meals, clothing, transportation (if a car is necessary, include repairs, insurance, fees, etc.), health insurance, education costs for children, and whatever else applies.

a. What is the difference between such a life and your own?

b. If someone lived such a basic economic life, where might it be at risk of failure?

c. What would be the potential hopes and worries of such a family?

7. In which economic group do you envision God? Why? Might another economic group envision God in another way?

SCRIPTURES/ECCLESIASTICUS

The poor use entreaties, but the rich answer roughly.

— Proverbs 18:23

A rich person does wrong, and even adds insults; a poor person suffers wrong, and must add apologies. When the rich person totters, he is supported by friends, but when the humble falls, he is pushed away even by friends. If the rich person slips, many come to the rescue; he speaks unseemly words, but they justify him. If the humble person slips, they even criticize him; he talks sense, but is not given a hearing. The rich person speaks and all are silent; they extol to the clouds what he says. The poor person speaks and they say, "Who is this fellow?" And should he stumble, they even push him down. Riches are good if they are free from sin; poverty is evil only in the opinion of the ungodly.

— Ecclesiasticus 13:3, 21–24

"Now his elder son was in the field; and when he came and approached the house, he heard music and dancing. He called one of the slaves and asked what was going on. He replied, 'Your brother has come, and your father has killed the fatted calf, because he has got him back safe and sound.' Then he became angry and refused to go in. His father came out and began to plead with him. But he answered his father, 'Listen! For all these years I have been working like a slave for you, and I have never disobeyed your command; yet you have never given me even a young goat so that I might celebrate with my friends. But when this son of yours came back, who has devoured your property with prostitutes, you killed the fatted calf for him!' Then the father said to him, 'Son, you are always with me, and all that is mine is yours. But we had to celebrate and rejoice, because this brother of yours was dead and has come to life; he was lost and has been found.' "

— Luke 15:25–32

[Among the more obvious examples of the existence of hidden rules is the difficulty of forgiveness for the sins of other classes. Among the middle class, the typical sins of the poor and of the rich can seem especially egregious. The thought sometimes is that any sin that I have not yet committed must be an especially bad one.]

"Two men went up to the temple to pray, one a Pharisee and the other a tax collector. The Pharisee, standing by himself, was praying thus, 'God, I thank you that I am not like other people: thieves, rogues, adulterers, or even like this tax collector. I fast twice a week; I give a tenth of all my income.' But the tax collector, standing far off, would not even look up to heaven, but was beating his breast and saying, 'God, be merciful to me, a sinner!' I tell you, this man went down to his home justified rather than the other; for all who exalt themselves will be humbled, but all who humble themselves will be exalted."

— Luke 18:10–14

Hidden Rules Among Classes

A Story

Sally was determined this morning. Don still wanted nothing to do with it, but she was going to that church today . . . even if she had to carry the two kids on her back.

Though the boys had not protested all that much, dressing had taken longer than expected. What few nice things they had were outgrown or nearly so. In the end, Tommy's worn jeans had to do. The dress Sally put on was the only thing she had for any such occasion. As they lined up in the hall to leave, the obvious problem was shoes; all the footwear looked pretty tired. But that could not matter, they had to go, now!

They could still make it on time, but Sally had hoped to be early. She hoped to see the way things were laid out before everyone arrived. The walk was not far and rather pleasant in a way. The church seemed a friendly building. Right beside the neighborhood, it was one of her favorite parts of moving there. In the months since she and Don had rented the house, she had wanted to visit the church. Only now things had settled down enough to try. Stepping up to the huge doors, she wondered what they were getting into.

It was a truly beautiful building, nicer than she remembered Grandma's church being. That small, wood-frame church was in a beautiful setting among a grove of old trees. But this was grand: strong stone walls, neatly cut lawn outlined with healthy shrubs, and everywhere a sense of "well cared for."

The service still had not begun as they walked into the vestibule. Just inside, Sally and the two boys met a friendly man who greeted them and noticed only that theirs were new faces. Yet, as they stepped into the sanctuary, others seemed to be noticing more. Everyone looked so nice—truly beautiful people. Sally thought of her dress. It hadn't seemed so short the last time she had worn it.

An usher offered to help them find a seat. Sally declined and started down a side aisle. They moved a few rows up the aisle and saw an opening. When they had almost sat down, a lady reached over the pew behind and suggested that the seats were taken. By that time Bobby did not want to move. Sally smiled as best she could and dragged the boys a few more rows forward. She found three seats there, in the middle of the pew. Sally wondered if the usher would have done better.

The service began with Sally preoccupied with her own self-consciousness. Thankfully, the boys were quiet, awed by the sanctuary's majestic trappings. The music was nice, and she knew one or two of the songs. The prayers and other words were not very easy to understand, but her senses were already too filled to notice. The sermon was good. She liked the preacher with the big smile and the strong voice. At one point in his lesson he made a comment about sin with which she strongly agreed. Like Grandma years ago, Sally shouted, "Amen!" Then it seemed that a hundred faces turned toward her. Even Tommy noticed.

Sally did not remember much of the rest of the service. The boys had become fidgety, and it took all she had to keep them marginally quiet. When it was over, Sally and the boys tried to work their way out quickly. Once or twice she thought of introducing herself, but the faces close by were always turned away. One man did talk a moment. He asked where they were from. She offered what she thought was a pleasantly ironic answer, that they only lived a block or so away. He seemed uninterested and moved on to another person. It was as though everyone had someone else they needed to talk to.

When Sally and the boys made it to the door, she turned them away from the parking-lot side of the building to walk the longer way home. She shushed the boys when they pointed this out. They didn't mind much, though. They had been freed from the too-quiet hour.

As she entered the house, Don called out, "How did it go?" Before answering, Sally thought, *Maybe it wasn't such a bad idea that Don stayed home.*

Hidden rules are the unspoken cues and habits of a group. Distinct cueing systems exist between and among groups and economic classes. Generally, in America, that notion is recognized for racial and ethnic groups, but not particularly for economic groups. There are many hidden rules to examine.

But first . . .

A LITTLE QUIZ

Take the quiz on the next three pages, putting a check mark by all the things you know how to do.

Could You Survive in Poverty?

Put a check by each item you know how to do.

☐ 1. I know which churches and sections of town have the best rummage sales.

☐ 2. I know which rummage sales have "bag sales" and when.

☐ 3. I know which grocery stores' garbage bins can be accessed for thrown-away food.

☐ 4. I know how to get someone out of jail.

☐ 5. I know how to physically fight and defend myself physically.

☐ 6. I know how to get a gun, even if I have a police record.

☐ 7. I know how to keep my clothes from being stolen at the Laundromat.

☐ 8. I know what problems to look for in a used car.

☐ 9. I know how to live without a checking account.

☐ 10. I know how to live without electricity and a phone.

☐ 11. I know how to use a knife as scissors.

☐ 12. I can entertain a group of friends with my personality and my stories.

☐ 13. I know what to do when I don't have money to pay the bills.

☐ 14. I know how to move in half a day.

☐ 15. I know how to get and use food stamps or an electronic card for benefits.

☐ 16. I know where the free medical clinics are.

☐ 17. I am very good at trading and bartering.

☐ 18. I can get by without a car.

Could You Survive in Middle Class?

Put a check by each item you know how to do.

❑   1.   I know how to get my children into Little League, piano lessons, soccer, etc.

❑   2.   I know how to properly set a table.

❑   3.   I know which stores are most likely to carry the clothing brands my family wears.

❑   4.   My children know the best name brands in clothing.

❑   5.   I know how to order in a nice restaurant.

❑   6.   I know how to use a credit card, checking account, and savings account—and I understand an annuity. I understand term life insurance, disability insurance, and 20/80 medical insurance policy, as well as house insurance, flood insurance, and replacement insurance.

❑   7.   I talk to my children about going to college.

❑   8.   I know how to get one of the best interest rates on my new-car loan.

❑   9.   I understand the difference among the principal, interest, and escrow statements on my house payment.

❑   10.   I know how to help my children with their homework and do not hesitate to call the school if I need additional information.

❑   11.   I know how to decorate the house for the different holidays.

❑   12.   I know how to get a library card.

❑   13.   I know how to use most of the tools in the garage.

❑   14.   I repair items in my house almost immediately when they break— or know a repair service and call it.

Could You Survive in Wealth?

Put a check by each item you know how to do.

❑ 1. I can read a menu in French, English, and another language.

❑ 2. I have several favorite restaurants in different countries of the world.

❑ 3. During the holidays, I know how to hire a decorator to identify the appropriate themes and items with which to decorate the house.

❑ 4. I know who my preferred financial advisor, legal service, designer, domestic-employment service, and hairdresser are.

❑ 5. I have at least two residences that are staffed and maintained.

❑ 6. I know how to ensure confidentiality and loyalty from my domestic staff.

❑ 7. I have at least two or three "screens" that keep people whom I do not wish to see away from me.

❑ 8. I fly in my own plane or the company plane.

❑ 9. I know how to enroll my children in the preferred private schools.

❑ 10. I know how to host the parties that "key" people attend.

❑ 11. I am on the boards of at least two charities.

❑ 12. I know the hidden rules of the Junior League.

❑ 13. I support or buy the work of a particular artist.

❑ 14. I know how to read a corporate financial statement and analyze my own financial statements.

The first point about this exercise is that if you fall mostly in the middle class, the assumption is that everyone knows these things. However, if you did not know many of the items for the other classes, the exercise points out how many of the hidden rules are taken for granted by a particular class, which assumes they are a given for everyone. What, then, are the hidden rules? The chart on pages 16 and 17 gives an overview of some of the major hidden rules among the classes of poverty, middle class, and wealth.

When an individual or family attempts to connect with a given church they do so with their personal list of needs, which they hope that church will meet. Those needs will at least partly be defined by things like the hidden rules on the following pages. Church leaders all hope for people who seek God from the purest motives. More often they see people who have other needs. It might be a poor woman seeking security from financial problems. A middle-class man, recently moved to town, might hope for initial sales contacts for his business. A wealthy family might want a base for displaying their abilities and talents. Many people, from all levels, just seek friends, but they hope for friends who know the rules.

Several additional explanations and stories may help explain parts of the quiz and chart. The bottom line or driving force against which decisions are made is important to note. For example, in one school district, the faculty had gone together to buy a refrigerator for a family who did not have one. About three weeks later, the children in the family were gone for a week. When the students returned, the teachers asked where they had been. The answer was that the family had gone camping because they were so stressed. What had they used for money to go camping? Proceeds from the sale of the refrigerator, of course. The bottom line in generational poverty is entertainment and relationships. In middle class, the criteria against which most decisions are made relate to work and achievement. In wealth, it is the ramifications of the financial, social, and political connections that have the weight.

Being able physically to fight or have someone who is willing to fight for you is important to survival in poverty. Yet, in middle class, being able to use

Hidden Rules Among Classes

	POVERTY
POSSESSIONS	People.
MONEY	To be used, spent.
PERSONALITY	Is for entertainment. Sense of humor is highly valued.
SOCIAL EMPHASIS	Social inclusion of people he/she likes.
FOOD	Key question: Did you have enough? Quantity important.
CLOTHING	Clothing valued for its individual style and expression of personality.
TIME	Present most important. Decisions made for moment based on feelings or survival.
EDUCATION	Valued and revered as abstract but not as reality.
DESTINY	Believes in fate. Cannot do much to mitigate chance.
LANGUAGE	Casual register. Language is about survival.
FAMILY STRUCTURE	Tends to be matriarchal.
WORLD VIEW	Sees world in terms of local setting.
LOVE	Love and acceptance conditional and based upon whether individual is liked.
DRIVING FORCES	Survival, relationships, entertainment.
HUMOR	About people and sex.

MIDDLE CLASS	WEALTH
Things.	One-of-a-kind objects, legacies, pedigrees.
To be managed.	To be conserved, invested.
Is for acquisition and stability. Achievement is highly valued.	Is for connections. Financial, political, social connections are highly valued.
Emphasis is on self-governance and self-sufficiency.	Emphasis is on social exclusion.
Key question: Did you like it? Quality important.	Key question: Was it presented well? Presentation important.
Clothing valued for its quality and acceptance into norm of middle class. Label important.	Clothing valued for its artistic sense and expression. Designer important.
Future most important. Decisions made against future ramifications.	Traditions and history most important. Decisions made partially on basis of tradition and decorum.
Crucial for climbing success ladder and making money.	Necessary tradition for making and maintaining connections.
Believes in choice. Can change future with good choices now.	Noblesse oblige.
Formal register. Language is about negotiation.	Formal register. Language is about networking.
Tends to be patriarchal.	Depends on who has money.
Sees world in terms of national setting.	Sees world in terms of international view.
Love and acceptance conditional and based largely upon achievement.	Love and acceptance conditional and related to social standing and connections.
Work, achievement.	Financial, political, social connections.
About situations.	About social faux pas.

words as tools to negotiate conflict is crucial. Many times in poverty the fists are used because the words are neither available nor respected.

One of the biggest difficulties in getting out of poverty is managing money and just the general information base around money. How can you manage something you've never had? Money is seen in poverty as an expression of personality and is used for entertainment and relationships. The notion of using money for security is truly grounded in the middle and wealthy classes.

The question in the quiz about using a knife as scissors was put there to illustrate the lack of tools available to those in poverty. Tools in many ways are one of the identifiers of middle class—from the kitchen to the garage. Therefore, the notion of maintaining property and repairing items is dependent upon having tools. When they are not available, things are not repaired or maintained. Students do not have access to scissors, pens, paper, pencils, rulers, etc., which may be part of an assignment.

One of the biggest differences among the classes is how "the world" is defined for them. Wealthy individuals view the international scene as their world. As one said, "My favorite restaurant is in Brazil." Middle class tends to see the world in terms of a national picture, while poverty sees the world in its immediate locale.

In wealth, to be introduced or accepted, one must have an individual already approved by that group make the introductions. Yet to stand back and not introduce yourself in a middle-class setting is not the accepted norm. And in poverty it is not unusual to have a comment made about the individual before he/she is ever introduced.

The discussion could continue about hidden rules. The key point is that hidden rules govern so much of our immediate assessment of an individual and his/her capabilities. These are often the factors that keep an individual from moving upward in a career—or even getting the position in the first place.

HOW THESE CHARACTERISTICS SURFACE WITH ADULTS AND CHILDREN FROM POVERTY

Place a check mark in front of the items that describe children or adults with whom you regularly interact. They ...

- ❑ get mad and quit their job/work. If they don't like the boss/teacher, they will quit. The emphasis is on the current feeling, not the long-term ramifications.

- ❑ will work hard if they like you.

- ❑ do not use conflict-resolution skills, preferring to settle issues in verbal or physical assaults or with humor.

- ❑ use survival language, tending to operate out of casual register.

- ❑ are not emotionally reserved when angry, usually saying exactly what is on their mind.

- ❑ have an extreme freedom of speech, enjoy a sense of humor, use the personality to entertain, have a love of stories about people.

- ❑ are very independent. They won't take kindly to the "parent" voice. If their full cooperation is sought, the boss/employer needs to use the "adult" voice.

- ❑ periodically need time off or late arrival due to family emergencies.

- ❑ need emotional warmth from colleagues/boss/teacher(s) in order to feel comfortable.

- ❑ require a level of integrity from management, actively distrusting organizations and the people who represent the organizations. They see organizations as basically dishonest.

❑ exhibit a possessiveness about the people they really like.

❑ need a greater amount of "space" to allow for the uniqueness of their personalities.

❑ show favoritism for certain people and give them preferential treatment.

Also . . .

■ Men socialize with men and women with women. Men tend to have two social outlets: bars and work. Women with children tend to stay at home and have only other female relatives as friends, unless they work outside the home. Men tend to be loners in any other social setting and avoid those social settings. When a man and a woman are together, it is usually about a private relationship.

■ A real man is ruggedly good-looking, is a lover, can physically fight, works hard, "takes no prisoners."

■ A real woman takes care of her man by feeding him and downplaying his shortcomings.

NOTE: In generational poverty, the primary role of a real man is to physically work hard, to be a fighter, and to be a lover. In middle class, a real man is a provider. If one follows the implications of a male identity as one who is a fighter and a lover, then one can understand why the male who takes this identity (of fighter and lover as his own) cannot have a stable life. Of the three responses to life—to flee, flow, or fight—he can only fight or flee. So when the stress gets high, he fights, then flees from the law and the people closest to him, leaving his home. Either way he is gone. When the heat dies down, he returns— to an initial welcome, then more fights. The cycle begins again.

CAN YOU IDENTIFY YOUR CHURCH?

Put a check by each item that describes your church.

❑   1.   I go to a church with a full-time worship coordinator.

❑   2.   I go to a church where the choir struggles.

❑   3.   I go to a church where the music is all congregational.

❑   4.   I give money to the church by check through a pledge.

❑   5.   I give money to the church in the offering. I am a good steward with my money.

❑   6.   I always give cash at church and as much as I can because Jesus is my friend.

❑   7.   The sermon is very emotional and often tear-based.

❑   8.   Prayers are participatory.

❑   9.   The sermon very often stresses beliefs and morals.

❑   10.   The sermon is philosophical and open-ended and is intended to promote thinking. Sources other than religious sources are used.

❑   11.   Sunday school class is mixed gender.

❑   12.   At our socials, the presentation of food is very important.

❑   13.   Our preacher is a man of God sent to lead his flock. He has little formal education.

❑   14.   At our socials, the quantity of food is very important.

❑   15. Our minister has had some college and has been to Bible college.

❑   16. At our socials, the quality of food is very important.

❑   17. Our minister is highly educated, both in liberal arts and advanced degrees in theology.

❑   18. Scriptural interpretation is based upon personal understanding.

❑   19. Scriptural interpretation is based upon years of study, using both Hebrew and Greek original texts.

❑   20. Our church has an altar call every Sunday, and in church we talk about witnessing to our friends and neighbors.

❑   21. Our church has a mission it supports in another part of the world. We urge those who would like to be saved to come forward and meet with the minister after church.

❑   22. Our church has several causes it supports worldwide and encourages those who would like to join the church to speak with the minister privately.

❑   23. Our church is mostly organized around the preacher. We have some men we call deacons or elders. The preacher is self-supporting.

❑   24. Our church is organized through a church council elected by the membership. The minister is hired by the church council and given a salary.

❑   25. Our church has a minister of music.

❑   26. Our church has a youth minister.

❏ 27. Our church is linked to a larger denominational organization to which we send money.

❏ 28. Our church has additions dedicated to particular families.

❏ 29. Our church has pews that are labeled and have been donated by an individual or family.

❏ 30. Our minister is often asked to offer prayers at political and government functions.

❏ 31. Our church is frequently requested as a site by non-members to hold a wedding.

❏ 32. Hell, fear, and punishment are stressed in our church. The Devil is often referenced.

❏ 33. Heaven, forgiveness, and love are stressed in our church. Hell is rarely mentioned and then only conceptually.

❏ 34. Heaven is to be sought after; hell is to be avoided.

❏ 35. Our church has a fellowship hall.

❏ 36. Our church has a gymnasium.

❏ 37. Our church has an urban ministry.

❏ 38. Our church has a choir.

❏ 39. We encourage our minister to drop in at any time.

❏ 40. Our minister calls before he/she comes to visit.

❏ 41. Our minister makes an appointment to meet with us— checking both our calendars.

❑ 42. When we pray for our prayer requests, we openly pray for God's healing through His personal touch.

❑ 43. When we pray for our prayer requests, we ask for God's blessing and healing and that God will guide the doctors and nurses.

❑ 44. The music that is part of the church service is participatory, often accompanied by clapping, guitars, etc. The congregation sings along.

❑ 45. The music that is part of the church service is traditional, often written 200 or more years ago; it usually comes from hymnals. The congregation sings along.

❑ 46. The music that is part of the church service is classical or baroque by well-known composers; it is often performed by trained musicians.

QUESTIONS

1. Have you ever shared a meal in a home from another economic group? What mistakes did you make? Is there any way you could have known better?

2. Which skills of other groups do you wish you had?

3. Try to think of some of the hidden rules that exist in a given church gathering. Consider appropriate entry and exit, seating, greeting etiquette, subjects of conversation that are acceptable and unacceptable.

4. When you have to spend time in a concentration of people from another economic group, are you uncomfortable? Why?

The hidden-rules chart on pages 26–29 is the church-based equivalent of the overall hidden-rules chart on pages 16 and 17.

Hidden Rules in Church

ISSUE	POVERTY
VIEW OF GIVING	Gives disproportionately in relation to income. Gives because Jesus is their friend. Gives cash.
VIEW OF CHARITY	Usually helps friends by giving them money or physical help.
CHURCH FINANCES	No written budget. No written record of offerings is kept.
PRAYER	Led by minister. Participatory and personal. Requests for healing part of prayer.
SERMONS	In casual register. Story-based. Often emotional. Frequent references to Devil. Scripture used for emphasis. Often fear-based. ("Do this or you will go to hell.")
MINISTER	Has little formal education. Has been called by God. Usually self-supporting.
SCRIPTURAL INTERPRETATION	Based on personal understanding. Doctrine can evolve almost weekly.
MISSION WORK	Involves personal testimony. Is neighborhood- and friend-based.

NOTE: *Few churches are totally in one column.*

MIDDLE CLASS	WEALTH
Often tithes. To give 10% is to be good steward. Gives in cash or check.	Money given by pledge through check. Special donations made for particular causes are often huge.
Prefers to give time to activities and events to help less fortunate. Concern about limited resources makes for careful commitment to projects, often for very long periods of time.	Time and money are given to assist with causes.
Written record of offerings and church expenditures. Budgets are established. Financial planning is used to build facilities.	Financial planning for operations is used, as well as for buildings. Projected costs are determined. Pledges are received from members to meet costs.
Offered by minister. General ("bless those who are sick") in orientation.	Often done through liturgy. Highly stylized.
In formal register. Sermon formulated around scriptural passage. Key points are extracted. Often future-based. ("You need to do this so you can go to heaven.")	In formal register. Philosophical in approach and is intended to promote positive thinking. Scripture is cited. Sources outside religion are used as well. ("In many ways, heaven and hell are states of mind.")
Usually has college degree and some formal theological training. Feels need to serve. Receives salary from church.	Highly educated. Often holds doctoral degree in theology. Is salaried by church. Often receives money from book sales, appointed positions, etc.
Doctrine stabilized by denominational leadership and living memories of senior members. Scholarship used more often to defend old than to introduce new.	Serious scholarship expected. More loosely tied to traditional doctrine. Leader congregations are more inclined to novel approaches to Scripture and issues.
Formally adopts mission site, usually in foreign country or urban area, which is supported with prayers and money.	Adopts and addresses causes, nationally and internationally, which are given financial support.

Hidden Rules in Church (CONTINUED)

ISSUE	POVERTY
YOUTH MINISTRY	Activities are loosely organized and sporadic.
SOCIAL EVENTS	Involves getting together and eating. Quantity of food important. Everyone brings dish.
ORGANIZATION OF THE CHURCH	Organized around charisma and personality of preacher.
JOINING THE CHURCH	Altar call is issued every Sunday.
CHURCH FACILITIES	Often older building is converted to use as church. Starts small.
NATURE OF SERVICE	Very emotional. Does not necessarily start on time. Follows general pattern announced by preacher as service progresses.
INSTRUMENTS FOR MUSIC	Recorded music.
MUSIC LEADERSHIP	Music activities provided by individuals who are interested in music. Music is selected on basis of personal or emotional reasons.
PURPOSE FOR COMING TO CHURCH	For relief and support. To receive emotional and spiritual rejuvenation.

MIDDLE CLASS	WEALTH
Activities are planned and continuous. Youth leadership is delegated to individuals.	Has youth director who coordinates and leads activities. Receives salary from church.
Involves program and food. Quality of food important. Main meat dish is often provided by church organization. Other food is brought by parishioners.	Highly planned, often using themes. Presentation of food and artistic quality of event important. Often organized to promote cause or event.
Organized through denomination. Follows guidelines of conference or district of denomination.	Flagship for denomination. Often provides leadership to denomination. Seen as not having to follow all guidelines of denomination.
Encourages those who would like to be saved and join church to meet with minister.	Encourages those who would like to join church to make appointment with minister to discuss.
Has church building that includes sanctuary and rooms for Sunday school meetings. May have area for social gathering ("Fellowship Hall").	Has church building with sanctuary, meeting rooms, social area, and sometimes gymnasium. Non-members often request facilities for weddings, social events, etc.
Follows written schedule, which is given to each person in bulletin. Expects that individuals will read and follow along. Service generally begins on time.	Follows written schedule in bulletin. Choices in service are made in terms of historical, literary, religious, or artistic merit. Professional musician(s) have part in service.
Piano.	Pipe organ.
Music activities overseen by individual(s) who have some musical training. Music is selected using denominational hymnbooks and personal knowledge about music.	Has director of music who is trained and degreed as professional. Music is selected for its historical, artistic, or religious merit. Composer, writer, and history of music are very important in selection.
For sense of well-being. To provide positive role model for children. To receive emotional and spiritual rejuvenation.	To make connections. To provide leadership role in community. To receive emotional and spiritual rejuvenation.

SCRIPTURES/ECCLESIASTICUS

I thank God that I speak in tongues more than all of you; nevertheless, in church I would rather speak five words with my mind, in order to instruct others also, than ten thousand words in a tongue. Tongues, then, are a sign not for believers but for unbelievers, while prophecy is not for unbelievers but for believers. If, therefore, the whole church comes together and all speak in tongues, and outsiders or unbelievers enter, will they not say that you are out of your mind? But if all prophesy, an unbeliever or outsider who enters is reproved by all and called to account by all. After the secrets of the unbeliever's heart are disclosed, that person will bow down before God and worship him, declaring, "God is really among you."

— 1 Corinthians 14:18–19, 22–25

[The issues around tongues speaking are many and complicated. What matters here is whether or not one is understood!]

When I came to you, brothers and sisters, I did not come proclaiming the mystery of God to you in lofty words or wisdom. For I decided to know nothing among you except Jesus Christ, and him crucified. And I came to you in weakness and in fear and in much trembling. My speech and my proclamation were not with plausible words of wisdom, but with a demonstration of the Spirit and of power, so that your faith might rest not on human wisdom but on the power of God.

— 1 Corinthians 2:1–5

To make an apt answer is a joy to anyone, and a word in season, how good it is!

— Proverbs 15:23

One who is clever conceals knowledge, but the mind of a fool broadcasts folly.

— Proverbs 12:23

When a sieve is shaken, the refuse appears; so do a person's faults when he speaks.

— Ecclesiasticus 27:4

{ CHAPTER 3 }

Language Patterns and Cognition

A Story

Preacher Clint sat at his desk, prepared to review his radio scripts. These were among the more challenging aspects of his ministry—and often his favorite too. He delighted in the idea of talking to large numbers of people and sharing with them the blessings of life with God. But there were complications in speaking as only a voice, and this forced him to be all the more clear. There were no gestures or facial expressions to clarify his meaning, only words. Also, there was no audience response. He could not know when to back up and restate. Each listener would take from his broadcast whatever he or she found. For the most part Clint never knew what that was.

Each week Clint's secretary transcribed a tape he made. He used those transcriptions to prepare his final recording. It was helpful for him to read her typed pages to see how she heard what he said. This week's manuscript was especially revealing. She'd had a little trouble understanding Clint at one point: "Let us consider the words of Paul in the ax of the apostles, chapter 13 . . ." What had Preacher Clint meant?

To better understand poverty, one must understand three aspects of language: registers of language, discourse patterns, and story structure. Many of the key issues for churches are related to these three patterns that often are different in poverty than they are in middle class.

REGISTERS OF LANGUAGE

Every language in the world has five registers (Joos, 1967). These registers are the following:

REGISTER	EXPLANATION
FROZEN	Language that is always the same. For example: Lord's Prayer, wedding vows, etc.
FORMAL	The standard sentence syntax and word choice of work and school. Has complete sentences and specific word choice.
CONSULTATIVE	Formal register when used in conversation. Discourse pattern not quite as direct as formal register.
CASUAL	Language between friends and is characterized by a 400- to 800-word vocabulary. Word choice general and not specific. Conversation dependent upon non-verbal assists. Sentence syntax often incomplete.
INTIMATE	Language between lovers or twins. Language of sexual harassment.

RULE: Joos found that one can go one register down in the same conversation, and that is socially accepted. However, to drop two registers or more in the same conversation is to be socially offensive.

How then does this register impact individuals from poverty? First of all, the work of Dr. Maria Montano-Harmon (1991) found that the majority of poor children do not have access to formal register at home. As a matter of fact, their parents cannot use formal register. The problem is that many sermons, Sunday school materials, etc., are in formal register.

It is further complicated by the fact that to get a well-paying job it is expected that one will be able to use formal register. Ability to use formal register is a hidden rule of the middle class. The inability to use it will knock one out of an interview in two or three minutes. The use of formal register, on the other hand, allows one to score well on tests and do well in higher education.

Few individuals in poverty have the vocabulary or the knowledge of sentence structure and syntax to use formal register. When student conversations in casual register are observed, much of the meaning comes not from the word choices, but from the non-verbal assists. To be asked to communicate in writing without the non-verbal assists is an overwhelming and formidable task, which most of them try to avoid. It has very little meaning for them.

PATTERNS OF DISCOURSE

In the oral-language tradition in which casual register operates, the pattern of discourse is quite different. Discourse is defined as the organizational pattern of information (see graphic representations below and on next page).

Formal-Register Discourse Pattern

Speaker or writer gets straight to the point.

Casual-Register Discourse Pattern

Writer or speaker goes around the issue before finally coming to the point.

This discourse pattern is coupled with a third pattern, that of story structure.

STORY STRUCTURE

Formal-Register Story Structure

The formal-register story structure starts at the beginning of the story and goes to the end in a chronological or accepted narrative pattern. The most important part of the story is the plot.

Casual-Register Story Structure

The casual-register story structure begins with the end of the story first or the part with the greatest emotional intensity. The story is told in vignettes, with audience participation in between. The story ends with a comment about the character and his/her value. The most important part of the story is the characterization.

Casual-register story structure is far more entertaining, more participatory, and exhibits a richness of character, humor, and feeling that is absent from formal register. Formal register has sequence, order, cause and effect, and a conclusion: all skills necessary for problem-solving, inference, etc.

Cognitive studies indicate that story structure is one way that the brain stores memories. Given the formal-register story structure, memories would be stored more sequentially, and thinking patterns would follow story structure. Feuerstein (1980) describes the episodic, nearly random memory of casual register and its adverse effects on thinking.

HOW DOES CASUAL-REGISTER STORY STRUCTURE AFFECT COGNITION?

If an individual depends upon a random, episodic story structure for memory patterns, lives in an unpredictable environment, and *has not developed the ability to plan,* then . . .

If an individual cannot plan, he/she *cannot predict.*

If an individual cannot predict, he/she *cannot identify cause and effect.*

If an individual cannot identify cause and effect, he/she *cannot identify consequence.*

If an individual cannot identify consequence, he/she *cannot control impulsivity.*

If an individual cannot control impulsivity, he/she *has an inclination toward criminal behavior.*

HOW DOES THIS AFFECT CHURCHES?

- Crucial in the transition from poverty to middle class is the acquisition of certain cognitive skills—particularly the ability to plan (one cannot control impulsivity without it) and the ability to ask questions that are grammatically correct or in English's formal register. It is the lack of planning that gets so many individuals in poverty in trouble financially, as well as behaviorally. To help individuals make the transition, churches must offer very tangible support in planning—both budgets and daily life.

At least one fellowship sends out planners to each church family to help design the household budget. To many individuals, this is invasive and unacceptable. However, in one-to-one relationships it is more acceptable.

■ The ability to link time and task is also missing in poverty. Therefore, the amount of time a task might take, the self-talk, and the procedures necessary to do the task also must be a part of the planning.

QUESTIONS

1. In what kinds of settings do you change your speech patterns? In front of your children/grandchildren? Your boss? At a sporting-goods store? At a library?

2. What kinds of different speech patterns can you find in the Bible? There are some interestingly different ones—e.g., some of the language of the Bible is rather simple (the writing of the apostle John), while in other places the vocabulary is quite advanced. The Psalms are usually very emotive. Paul's letters are often logically tight and require careful concentration.

3. Take a look at an employment form or application for business agreement. Who is trying to communicate with whom? When an individual comes to a church and is asked to fill out a form, what is that form like? Are you reaching out to them, or are you asking the person to come to where you stand?

SCRIPTURES/ECCLESIASTICUS

It is honorable to refrain from strife, but every fool is quick to quarrel.

– Proverbs 20:3

Do not get angry with your neighbor for every injury, and do not resort to acts of insolence.

– Ecclesiasticus 10:6

For lack of wood the fire goes out, and where there is no whisperer, quarreling ceases.

– Proverbs 26:20

In proportion to the fuel, so will the fire burn, and in proportion to the obstinacy, so will strife increase; in proportion to a person's strength will be his anger, and in proportion to his wealth he will increase his wrath. A hasty quarrel kindles a fire, and a hasty dispute sheds blood. If you blow on a spark, it will glow; if you spit on it, it will be put out; yet both come out of your mouth.

– Ecclesiasticus 28:10–12

For the whole law is summed up in a single commandment, "You shall love your neighbor as yourself." If, however, you bite and devour one another, take care that you are not consumed by one another.

– Galatians 5:14–15

And the Lord's servant must not be quarrelsome but kindly to everyone, an apt teacher, patient, correcting opponents with gentleness. God may perhaps grant that they will repent and come to know the truth, and that they may escape from the snare of the devil, having been held captive by him to do his will.

– 2 Timothy 2:24–26

{ CHAPTER 4 }

Violence/Conflict Resolution

Just then a lawyer stood up to test Jesus. "Teacher," he said, "what must I do to inherit eternal life?" He said to him, "What is written in the law? What do you read there?" He answered, "You shall love the Lord your God with all your heart, and with all your soul, and with all your strength, and with all your mind; and your neighbor as yourself." And he said to him, "You have given the right answer; do this, and you will live." But wanting to justify himself, he asked Jesus, "And who is my neighbor?" Jesus replied, "A man was going down from Jerusalem to Jericho, and fell into the hands of robbers, who stripped him, beat him, and went away, leaving him half dead. Now by chance a priest was going down that road; and when he saw him, he passed by on the other side. So likewise a Levite, when he came to the place and saw him, passed by on the other side. But a Samaritan while traveling came near him; and when he saw him, he was moved with pity. He went to him and bandaged his wounds, having poured oil and wine on them. Then he put him on his own animal, brought him to an inn, and took care of him. The next day he took out two denarii, gave them to the innkeeper, and said, 'Take care of him; and when I come back, I will repay you whatever more you spend.' Which of these three, do you think, was a neighbor to the man who fell into the hands of the robbers?" He said, "The one who showed him mercy." Jesus said to him, "Go and do likewise."

– Luke 10:25–37

[Basic to the story is the understood hatred of the Jews (especially the upper-class Jews) against the hero's people, the Samaritans.]

A Story

Quinton loved his new bicycle. He hadn't had many new things before.
Even if he didn't appreciate all that it had cost his mom, he knew that is was
special beyond anything he owned.

He also knew that there were risks when he rode it to the store. The guys
in the neighborhood would probably not mess with him, but you never knew.
There were a few of them around when he got to the store and went inside.
It was only as he came out that he saw the three strange boys. They were
standing around his bike. One of them was sitting on it. They weren't all that
big. They just looked at Quinton, then rode it away.

He hadn't been afraid. At least he thought he wasn't afraid. No, the
reason he hadn't fought had to do with what Preacher John had been saying.
Preacher John talked a lot about Jesus. Jesus didn't like fighting, and Quinton
had promised himself that he was going to quit fighting. Quinton didn't
know what Jesus had lost when he hadn't fought, but he had seen Preacher
John lose stuff That bicycle was the best thing Quinton had ever had. He went
home hurting and confused.

His mom wasn't confused though. "Lord, have mercy! That bicycle cost
a bundle. "She gave Quinton a hard beating and sent him outside. It wasn't
just the bicycle. "If that boy won't take care of a bicycle," she said aloud to no
one in particular, "will he take care of himself? Will he take care of his sister?
Wait till I talk to that preacher."

To understand the neighborhoods of poverty, it is crucial to understand
the role of violence. Physical violence occurs in part because of the lack of
abstract language in casual register and the fighter/lover identity of many
of the men in generational poverty. A real man fights. The heroes of the
stories in generational poverty tend to be trickster heroes and anti-heroes
(e.g., Robin Hood).

One of the reasons parents don't want their children to leave is so that

they are physically protected in their old age. Old people need physical protection in generational-poverty neighborhoods.

In most churches, physical fighting is neither condoned nor admired.
It is usually condoned only if it's part of the occupation (police work, etc.)
or involved in military service.

SUGGESTIONS

- Do not rule out physical fighting or disparage it. Simply teach
  other methods to try first. Humor is often the technique used to
  lessen physical fighting.

- Have wives ask their husbands to bring them and the children to
  church (even if the husband does not attend) so that the men feel
  validated in their role of keeping the women and children safe.

- Provide after-school classes in karate, judo, etc., because they
  teach discipline and self-restraint while also providing a method
  of self-defense.

- Teach the adult voice.

THE LANGUAGE OF NEGOTIATION

One of the biggest issues with people from poverty is the fact that many
children in poverty must function as their own parents. They parent themselves and others—often younger siblings. In many instances they also act
as parent to the adult in the household.

Inside virtually everyone's head are three internal voices that guide the
individual. These voices are the child voice, the adult voice, and the parent
voice. It has been our observation that individuals who have become their
own parent quite young do not have an internal adult voice. They have a
child voice and a parent voice, but not an adult voice.

An internal adult voice allows for negotiation. This voice provides the language of negotiation and allows issues to be examined in a non-threatening way.

Many church people tend to speak to individuals in a parent voice, particularly in discipline situations. To the person who already is functioning as a parent, this is unbearable. Almost immediately, the situation is exacerbated beyond the original incident. The tendency for church members to use the parent voice with individuals who are poor is based on the assumption that a lack of resources must indicate a lack of intelligence. Individuals in poverty are very offended by this.

When the parent voice is used with an individual from poverty, the outcome is frequently anger. He/she is angry because anger is based on fear. What the parent voice forces the individual to do is use either the child voice or the parent voice. If the person from poverty uses the parent voice, which could sound sarcastic in this context, the individual will get into trouble. If the individual uses the child voice, he/she will feel helpless and therefore at the mercy of the church member. Many individuals choose to use the parent voice because it is less frightening than memories connected with being helpless.

Part of the reality of poverty is the language of survival. There are simply not enough resources for people in poverty to engage in a discussion of them. For example, if there are five hot dogs and five people, the distribution of the food is fairly clear. The condiments for the hot dogs are going to be limited, so the discussion about their distribution will be fairly limited as well. Contrast that, for example, with a middle-class household where the discussion will be about how many hot dogs, what should go on the hot dog, how much of each ingredient, etc. Thus the ability to see options and to negotiate among those options is not well-developed in poverty.

To teach individuals to use the "language of negotiation" one must first teach them the phrases they can use. Have them use the "adult" voice in discussions. Direct-teach the notion of an adult voice, and give them phrases to use. Have them tally each time they use a phrase from the "adult" voice.

There will be laughter. However, over time, if church members also model that voice in interactions with individuals from poverty, one will hear more of those kinds of questions and statements.

In addition to this strategy, several training programs are available to teach peer negotiation. It is important that, as part of the negotiation, the culture of origin is not denigrated, but rather the ability to negotiate is seen as a survival tool for the work, school, and church setting.

Adapted from the work of Eric Berne

THE CHILD VOICE *
Defensive, victimized, emotional, whining, losing attitude, strongly negative non-verbal.

- Quit picking on me.
- You don't love me.
- You want me to leave.
- Nobody likes (loves) me.
- I hate you.
- You're ugly.
- You make me sick.
- It's your fault.
- Don't blame me.
- She, he, _____ did it.
- You make me mad.
- You made me do it.

* *The child voice is also playful, spontaneous, curious, etc. The phrases listed often occur in conflictual or manipulative situations and impede resolution.*

THE PARENT VOICE * **
Authoritative, directive, judgmental, evaluative, win-lose mentality, demanding, punitive, sometimes threatening.

- You shouldn't (should) do that.

- It's wrong (right) to do _____ .

- That's stupid, immature, out of line, ridiculous.

- Life's not fair. Get busy.

- You are good, bad, worthless, beautiful (any judgmental, evaluative comment).

- You do as I say.

- If you weren't so _____ , this wouldn't happen to you.

- Why can't you be like _____ ?

* *The parent voice can also be very loving and supportive. The phrases listed usually occur during conflict and impede resolution.*

** *The internal parent voice can create shame and guilt.*

THE ADULT VOICE
Non-judgmental, free of negative non-verbal, factual, often in question format, attitude of win-win.

- In what ways could this be resolved?

- What factors will be used to determine the effectiveness, quality of _____ ?

- I would like to recommend _____ .

- What are choices in this situation?

- I am comfortable (uncomfortable) with _____ .

- Options that could be considered are _____ .

- For me to be comfortable, I need the following things to occur
  _____ .

- These are the consequences of that choice/action _____ .

- We agree to disagree.

VERBAL ABUSE

The parent voice leads to verbal abuse. Verbal abuse is subtle, negative,
and double-messaged. Patricia Evans, in her book *The Verbally Abusive
Relationship* (1992), identifies 15 different kinds of verbal abuse. Verbal
abuse prevents relationships of mutual respect from being developed.
Noted researcher Alice Miller states that individuals who are verbally abusive
are raised in a situation where the primary caregiver is *not* sympathetic or
empathetic to the needs of the individual.

Verbal abuse destroys relationships of mutual respect. *NOTE: Verbal
abuse is often used as a control mechanism. However, it builds latent hostility.*

Many of the following situations, in which the child or adult is speaking,
could relate to Sunday school or summer Bible school.

TYPE	DEFINITION	EXAMPLES
Withholding	To remain cool and indifferent, to be silent and aloof, to reveal as little as possible.	"What do you want me to say?" "Why should I care if you like it?" "I don't have to tell you how to do it." "I don't have to answer your question."
Countering	To express the opposite of what the person says.	"This assignment is hard." "No, it's not. It's easy." "You're not fair." "Yes, I am."
Discounting	To deny the experience of the other person.	"You don't know what you're talking about." "You think you know it all." "You're looking for a fight." "You're jumping to conclusions."

TYPE	DEFINITION	EXAMPLES
Disguised as a joke	To make disparaging comments disguised as a joke.	"You couldn't find your head if it wasn't attached." "You're so ugly even a mother couldn't love you." "When God was giving out brains, you thought he said trains, and you got in the wrong line!"
Blocking and diverting	To prevent the conversation from continuing, often by switching the topic.	"You're just trying to have the last word." "You heard me. I shouldn't have to repeat myself." "Did anybody ask you?" "Will you get off my back?"
Accusing and blaming	To blame the other person for one's own anger, irritation, or insecurity.	"You're looking for trouble." "You're just trying to pick a fight." "You don't care about me."
Judging and criticizing	To judge and express the judgment in a negative, critical way; to judge a third person and express it in a negative, critical way.	"You're stupid." "You're lazy." "You're an awful teacher." "She can't keep anything straight."
Trivializing	To diminish and make insignificant the work or contribution of the other person.	"I know you helped me do the problem, but you should have given me the answer." "I realize you did the work yourself, but did you have to write your name so big?"
Undermining	To dampen interest and enthusiasm by eroding confidence.	"Really, I don't know anyone who would be interested in that." "What makes you think you're so smart?" "Couldn't you find a more boring topic?" "Who are you trying to impress?" "Did you really go to college?"

TYPE	DEFINITION	EXAMPLES
Threatening	To manipulate by threatening loss or pain.	"Do that again and I'll kick you out." "My mom's going to call you." "You mess with me, and my dad will get you."
Name calling	To call the other person names, including terms of endearment that are said sarcastically.	"Well, darling . . ." "You're a —— !" "You're a troublemaker!"
Forgetting	To forget incidents, promises, and agreements for the purpose of manipulation.	"I don't know what you're talking about." "I never agreed to that!" "Where did you get that?" "I never promised to behave."
Ordering	To give orders instead of asking respectfully.	"Do your work and shut up." "Quit looking at me."
Denial	To deny the reality of the other person.	"You made that up." "You're crazy." "Where did you get that?" "I never said that. I never did that."
Abusive anger	To use anger, both verbally and non-verbally, in unpredictable outbursts to put the blame for his/her own inadequacies on the other person. It includes verbal rage, snapping at a person, and shouting. It is part of the anger-addiction cycle in which the person releases inner tension. It can be triggered by changes at home or school, fears, the current sense of power, feelings of dependency or inadequacy, or unmet needs.	Teacher: "Why didn't the home-work get done?" Student: "You're a —— !" (Gets up and stomps out of the room.) Student: "I don't understand." Teacher: Throws down the pencil and yells, "You never understand. Why are you in this class anyway?"

ELIMINATING VERBAL ABUSE

In order to eliminate verbal abuse, it must first be defined and recognized.

To build a relationship that is not verbally abusive, the following techniques need to be used and followed:

1. Use the adult voice.
2. Stop the abuse. Pivot the conversation to the issue.
3. Use silence.

Verbal abuse is the primary tool of emotional blackmail, which is the use of guilt, fear, or obligation to manipulate a person. Emotional blackmail must be stopped at the first demand.

EMOTIONAL COACHING

To emotionally coach, some guidelines are helpful.

DO	DON'T
Allow the individual to solve his/her own problems.	Try to fix the problem or the person.
Use the adult voice.	Use the parent voice.
Ask questions that allow the individual to examine the issue and the options.	Use verbal abuse.
Accept the individual's feelings.	Let the individual's feelings run or control the relationship.
Stop negative behaviors.	Become embroiled in a discussion with the individual about him/her that distracts from the situation at hand.

OBSERVATION

A Christian with a secure income and a number of stable relationships can look ahead to eternal issues with less worry about today. There are others who have more immediate concerns. Concerns about food, shelter, and especially personal safety can take a person's mind off matters no farther away than the class report due next week or the conference with Leo's teacher on Thursday. Eternity can seem a long way off.

There are parents whose young children must walk daily on dangerous streets. For them violence is not just the enemy, it may be their only hope for a secure path. Children who feel they have no friends among teachers and authorities must take care of their own safety. In such cases it can become a virtue, especially in the eyes of the parent, for a child to be a fighter. Older children are counted upon to take care of siblings. There may be no one else.

The concern is put simply: "Who's got your back?"

QUESTIONS

1. Who are your favorite characters in TV and movies? How do they usually resolve their problems?

2. Sports metaphors are a large part of our communication tools. Many of them are basically violent or at least imply the defeat of another. There are "crushing" victories. One team "destroys" another, although both walk away with all bones intact! A track star does not merely run faster than the others in a race, he "beats" them. Such are not reserved for sports alone, but are interlaced in our vocabularies, even in our sermons. The Bible itself uses plenty of violent language. How long would someone have to be around you and your Christian friends before they knew what you thought about violence?

3. The language of confrontation (in any particular situation) is greatly affected by who has the power position. Individuals don't demand much from their bosses. They need to be subtle and give careful requests. On the other hand, a supervisor can be quite free with directions or demands and need not be well-schooled in appropriate vocabulary. When dealing with a poor individual, are you as thoughtful as you are with another who is wealthier?

4. A good portion of gossip and slander goes on because people don't know how to effectively address someone they have a problem with. While we preach against gossip and slander, how much do we teach effective confrontation/communication skills?

SCRIPTURES

A friend loves at all times, and kinsfolk are born to share adversity.

— Proverbs 17:17

Jesus said to her, "Go, call your husband, and come back." The woman answered him, "I have no husband." Jesus said to her, "You are right in saying, 'I have no husband'; for you have had five husbands, and the one you have now is not your husband. What you have said is true!"

— John 4:16–18

Wives, be subject to your husbands as you are to the Lord. For the husband is the head of the wife just as Christ is the head of the church, the body of which he is the Savior. Just as the church is subject to Christ, so also wives ought to be, in everything, to their husbands. Husbands, love your wives, just as Christ loved the church and gave himself up for her, in order to make her holy by cleansing her with the washing of water by the word, so as to present the church to himself in splendor, without a spot or wrinkle or anything of the kind—yes, so that she may be holy and without blemish. In the same way, husbands should love their wives as they do their own bodies. He who loves his wife loves himself. For no one ever hates his own body, but he nourishes and tenderly cares for it, just as Christ does for the church, because we are members of his body. "For this reason a man will leave his father and mother and be joined to his wife, and the two will become one flesh." This is a great mystery, and I am applying it to Christ and the church. Each of you, however, should love his wife as himself, and a wife should respect her husband.

— Ephesians 5:22–33

[This is touchy stuff. Among the many concerns of some is that husbands in charge would inevitably abuse their wives. (The general body sizes of males and females makes abuse of wives a constant possibility.) The model offered is clearly pushing in another direction; love as Christ loved the church.]

{ CHAPTER 5 }

Family Structure and Marital Relationships

A Story

Randi sat down to fill out the form at the church food pantry. This was so embarrassing . . .

My spelling is terrible. And some of these questions . . . What did they want all this for? "What is your driver's license number?" "How long have you lived at this address?" It's like being back in school! "Marital status?" That's kind of hard to say this week. Terry's gone again . . . and who knows when he'll be back. "Do you want a visit from a minister?" Would that mean more help, or just more questions? "Who recommended that you come here for help?" Who do they want to recommend me? Who do they not want?

"Who lives with you in your home?" Let's see . . . There are the kids: Tommy, Sarah, Ruth. Terry has moved out; that's why I'm here! What if Bonnie comes back this weekend and brings the twins? . . .

FAMILY PATTERNS IN GENERATIONAL POVERTY

One of the most confusing things about understanding generational poverty is the family patterns. In the middle-class family, even with divorce, lineage is fairly easy to trace because of the legal documents. In generational poverty, on the other hand, many marital arrangements are common-law. Marriage and divorce in a legal court are important only if there is property to distribute or custody of children. When you were never legally married to begin with and you have no property, why pay a lawyer for something you don't have, don't need, and don't have the money to purchase?

In the middle class, family diagrams tend to be drawn in this fashion:

DIAGRAM OF MIDDLE-CLASS FAMILY

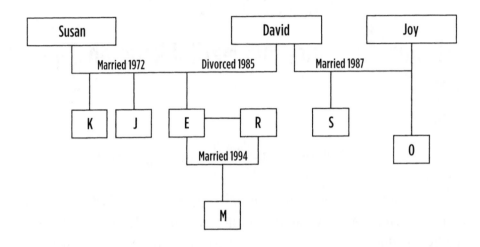

The notion is that lineage is traceable and that a linear pattern can be found.

In generational poverty, the mother is the center of the organization, and the family radiates from that center. Although it can happen that the mother is uncertain of the biological father, most of the time the father of the child is known. The pattern shown on the next page is based on a real situation. (Names have been changed.)

In this pattern, Jolyn has been legally married three times. Jolyn and Husband #1 had no children. Jolyn and Husband #2 had one child, Willy. They divorced. Husband #2 eventually married the woman he lived with for several years, and they had a child together. She also had a son from a previous marriage. Willy has a common-law wife, Shea; Shea and Willy have a daughter. Jolyn and Husband #3 lived together several years before they were married, and they have a son named M.J. When M.J. was 13 he had a child with a 13-year-old girl, but that child lives with the girl's mother. Husband #3 and Jolyn divorced; Jolyn is now living with a woman in a lesbian relationship. Husband #3 is living with a younger woman who is pregnant with his child.

**DIAGRAM OF FAMILY FROM
GENERATIONAL POVERTY**

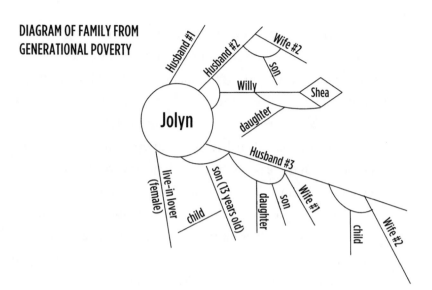

The mother is always at the center, though she may have multiple sexual relationships. Many of her children also will have multiple relationships, which may or may not produce children. The basic pattern is the mother at the heart of things, with nearly everyone having multiple relationships, some legal and some not. Eventually the relationships become intertwined. It wouldn't be out of the question for your sister's third husband to become your brother's ex-wife's live-in boyfriend. Also in this pattern are babies born out of wedlock to children in their early teens; these youngsters are often raised by the grandmother as her own children. For example, the oldest daughter has a child at 14. This infant becomes the youngest child in the existing family. The oldest daughter, who is actually the mother of the child, is referred to as her sister—and the relationship is a sibling one, not a mother-daughter one.

But the mother or maternal grandmother usually keeps her biological children. Because of the violence in poverty, death tends to be a prominent part of the family history. But it is also part of the family present because the deceased plays such a role in the memories of the family. It is important to note when dealing with the family patterns who is alive and who is dead—because in the discussions they are often still living (unless you, the listener, know differently).

Frequently, in stories that come to the attention of church people, the individual will tell the story in the episodic, random manner of the casual-register story structure. Key individuals are usually not referred to during the story because making reference to them isn't part of the story structure. *The most important keys to understanding the story are often the omissions.* For example, when someone says, "He left," you can pretty much predict who "he" will go stay with when there is trouble. If he is having trouble with his mother, he will go stay with an ex-wife or a girlfriend. If he is having trouble with his current wife, he will go stay with his mother. Women tend to go stay with their sisters and sometimes their mothers. Whether or not a mother or ex-wife is mentioned in the story, if the family is in generational poverty, you can be fairly certain that these are key players. You can also be fairly sure that the males are in and out—sometimes present, sometimes not, but not in any predictable pattern. Furthermore, you can know that as the male temporarily or permanently changes residences, the allegiances will change also.

Additionally within these families there tend to be multiple internal feuds. Allegiances may change overnight; favoritism is a way of life. *Who children go to stay with after school, who stays with whom when there is trouble, and who is available to deal with problems are dependent on the current alliances and relationships at that moment.* For example, Ned comes home drunk and beats up his wife, Susan. She calls the police and escapes with the three kids to her mother's house. He goes to his mother's because she arranges to get him out of jail. His mother is not speaking to Susan because she called the cops on him and put him in jail. But Ned's mother usually keeps his kids after school until Susan gets home. Now it is Monday, and Susan doesn't have any place to send the kids. So she tells them to go to her mother's house after school, which means they must go on a different bus because she doesn't know if Ned will show up at the house and be waiting for her. On Tuesday the kids again go to Susan's mom's house. But on Wednesday Ned's mom calls Susan and tells her that that no-good Ned got drunk last night and she kicked him out of her house. So now Susan and Ned's mother are good friends, and Ned is on the hot seat. So Ned goes to the apartment of his ex-wife, Jackie, because last week she decided she'd had enough of Jerry, and she was very glad to see Ned . . . And so the story continues.

The key roles in these families are fighter/lover, caretaker/rescuer, worker, storyteller, and "keeper of the soul" (i.e., dispenser of penance and forgiveness). The family patterns in generational poverty are different from the middle class. *In poverty the roles, the multiple relationships, the nature of the male identity, the ever-changing allegiances, the favoritism, and the matriarchal structure result in a different pattern.*

MARITAL RELATIONSHIPS

In middle class, marital relationships tend to be role-related. For example, a spouse is often referred to as a husband or a wife, a girlfriend or boyfriend, a fiancee.

But in poverty, the relationship is very sexual and gender-related. For example, "this is my woman," "this is my man."

Additionally, "rite of passage" (when adults in one's group consider adolescents or teens to be adults) differs by class. The middle-class rite of passage is about a job, graduation, driver's license, marriage, and military service. In generational poverty, rite of passage is to father or mother a child. In middle class, a teenager having a child is not viewed positively. In generational poverty, there is pride that one's children are potent or fertile. While the rhetoric against it may be harsh, the understanding is that it is expected.

Integral to understanding the marital relationship is to know the primary identity issue. When men go without work for long periods of time, male identity often changes from being a provider to being a fighter and lover. The corresponding female identity becomes a caretaker and a rescuer.

That is why, when a couple from poverty comes to a church to ask for assistance, the man will sit in the car while the woman comes in and asks. A fighter and lover is to protect and support (often unpredictably). But a woman is a rescuer and caretaker.

To understand the marital relationship in generational poverty, three things must be kept in mind: identity, casual register, and lack of adult voice. Because casual register has very few abstract words, and because the adult voice is usually missing, conversations often occur "in the concrete," and either the parent voice or child voice is used (which creates a power-oriented, win-lose relationship as opposed to a partnership). The relationship does not have a vehicle for resolving conflicts or issues. Very often the conflict starts over something concrete, gets personal, then becomes loaded with sexual innuendo, and finally turns violent.

Resolution to violence is limited to human fighting or walking out. (Sometimes a man will say, "I left so I wouldn't hit her.") Often when the male walks out, he walks to a local bar. As Willie Nelson sings, "The women all get prettier at closing time." He leaves with another woman or his buddies.

This scenario then becomes laden with the notion of punishment and forgiveness. Often both decide to punish the other—either by not allowing the other back in the house or by staying the night with another woman. Or the man may come back violent. The man (if he leaves) is "trashed" in the neighborhood, whereas he is a hero in the bar. The woman, meanwhile, is a heroine in the neighborhood. It becomes entertainment.

What does this do to the family?

It creates from day to day an unpredictable situation.

If the man comes back and has been violent, then when it's over the woman has the right to dispense punishment and forgiveness. Part of the punishment for a man may be to purchase something for the woman or, at the very least, take her some place, do as she says, or keep a low profile until he's forgiven.

Part of what happens in domestic violence is that whoever is in the parent voice generally "wins." However, if both male and female are in the parent voice, the one who is physically stronger usually wins.

The socialization process is that women tend to socialize with women and men with men. If you've ever been in a low-income neighborhood and have seen men standing in a circle drinking beer, they're socializing by almost certainly exchanging stories of their fighting and loving episodes.

THE PROCESS THAT HAPPENS WHEN THE RELATIONSHIP BREAKS

When a relationship breaks, it usually goes through a predictable process.

> **Anger**
>
> **Criticism**
>
> **Contempt**
>
> **Silence (withholding or avoidance)**
>
> **Separation**

Anger begins the process and leads to criticism. Criticism leads to contempt. Contempt leads to silence. If the silence continues, it leads to separation.

It is not unusual for anger, criticism, and contempt to be in the same interaction. The spouse or partner goes directly to separation and leaves the house.

After a relationship is broken, a period of transition occurs. There is new learning and consolidation of the learning. This next process occurs:

> **Loss of the relationship**
>
> **Grieving over the loss**
>
> **Change in self-image**
>
> **Learning of new skills (often with someone new)**
>
> **Practicing of new skills**

HOW DO THESE KINDS OF RELATIONSHIPS AFFECT CHURCHES?

■ Plans to attend change at the last minute. Excuses are given that make little sense.

■ Often children are involved in either caring for other children or in rescuing a parent. Neither situation can be explained.

■ Co-education of teen and adult Sunday school classes is not recommended initially. There is often jealousy and badgering if a woman is without the man in a mixed class.

■ Have activities that involve children. That way the woman can come to church without being badgered.

HOW CAN THE MARITAL RELATIONSHIP BE CHANGED?

■ Start with young males.

■ Provide resources and education for women.

■ Often men with fighter/lover identities do not attend church much between the ages of 18 and 45 to 50. It is difficult for them because they must give up key relationships and "drinking buddies." However, churches can get these men involved by doing the following:

  ▲ Offering classes (e.g., car repair).

  ▲ Making available athletic fields, exercise facilities, and team sports that men can be involved in with sons. Use family activities that include food. When the male is supportive he will not keep his children from attending.

■ Provide training for women and children about phrases and words to use in the adult voice that de-escalate violence.

- For example, in middle class, creating verbal and emotional distance, using ground rules, and focusing on the issue are all techniques used to lessen conflict.

- Study the book *Men Are from Mars, Women Are from Venus.*

- Develop relationships between church women and women in poverty neighborhoods. A point of common bond is the children. Note, however, that if a "fighter/lover" believes that his woman has changed too much, he will do everything he can to keep her from attending.

When counseling, understand the payoffs for both sides in the punishment / forgiveness routine.

OBSERVATIONS

A marriage is not just between two individuals, it's between two families. It can be between two cultures. The family pew had its purposes. Among them was a concern for appropriate marriage. Then and now what is at stake is the status of the next generation. Fear of cross-cultural (or interracial or trans-economic) marriage remains significant among the factors that divide people. Those who have a lot—and a lot to lose—are more likely to seek a safe distance from those they see as the "wrong" ethnic, cultural, and economic groups.

Churches ask many questions of people when they come for help. We know what we mean and why we ask so many questions, but can the folks seeking assistance have any understanding of the process (unless they've already been to other churches)?

QUESTIONS

1. Do a little research. How much does it cost to divorce? (Consider not only legal help, but also setting up a second household, transportation, children issues, etc.)

2. What are the advantages of a stable marriage to someone who has little money and no particular position in the community to defend? What might be considered disadvantages?

3. What does Christianity offer to a man who is asked to give up his recognized position of fighter/lover?

SCRIPTURES/ECCLESIASTICUS

Whoever is kind to the poor lends to the LORD, and will be repaid in full.

— Proverbs 19:17

The poor are disliked even by their neighbors, but the rich have many friends. Those who despise their neighbors are sinners, but happy are those who are kind to the poor.

— Proverbs 14:20–21

Riches are good if they are free from sin; poverty is evil only in the opinion of the ungodly.

— Ecclesiasticus 13:24

Someone in the crowd said to him, "Teacher, tell my brother to divide the family inheritance with me." But he said to him, "Friend, who set me to be a judge or arbitrator over you?" And he said to them, "Take care! Be on your guard against all kinds of greed; for one's life does not consist in the abundance of possessions." Then he told them a parable: "The land of a rich man produced abundantly. And he thought to himself, 'What should I do, for I have no place to store my crops?' Then he said, 'I will do this: I will pull down my barns and build larger ones, and there I will store all my grain and my goods. And I will say to my soul, 'Soul, you have ample goods laid up for many years; relax, eat, drink, be merry.' But God said to him, 'You fool! This very night your life is being demanded of you. And the things you have prepared, whose will they be?' So it is with those who store up treasures for themselves but are not rich toward God."

— Luke 12:13–21

Do not be deceived; God is not mocked, for you reap whatever you sow. If you sow to your own flesh, you will reap corruption from the flesh; but if you sow to the Spirit, you will reap eternal life from the Spirit. So let us not grow weary in doing what is right, for we will reap at harvest time, if we do not give up. So then, whenever we have an opportunity, let us work for the good of all, and especially for those of the family of faith.

— Galatians 6:7–10

{ CHAPTER 6 }

Money, Stewardship, and Spending

A Story

Scotty was 13, it was summer, and he needed a job. He had come to the church for a few years as one of the neighborhood kids. He had known for some time that his presence was less than completely welcomed by some, but he had friends too. One of them was the young minister, Drew. Scotty had asked him about the church's lawn and received an awkward answer he understood to be "No."

Drew knew that Scotty's request could not be accepted. Lawn mowers were admittedly dangerous. Questions of liability were all around, and no one knew nearly enough about Scotty's family. Still, Drew wanted to do better. Scotty was one of the "good" kids. The minister made several calls and finally lined up a pair of families who would give the kid a chance. Neither paid much, and Drew had to spend a couple of mornings training Scotty how to do the job. He even had to make a follow-up call or two about an assault on a rose bush. Basically, things went well enough. The reviews came back sufficient for a few more to give Scotty a try.

At the end of June, Scotty came by Drew's office with a strange request. Would Drew hold $75 for him? Scotty's answer to the question "Why?" left Drew unclear, but willing. The rest of the summer, more money came in, finally totaling over $350.

Just before school began, Scotty came in and asked for most of the money. Drew had wanted to advise Scotty on what to do. Surely he should take most of it and buy his own mower and some other equipment. At the very least he should buy some clothes for school. In the end Drew said nothing and hoped for the best.

When the next Sunday brought Scotty to services in the same old clothes, Drew imagined all sorts of foolish purchases. After worship Drew could stand it no longer and asked Scotty what he had done with the money.

Scotty looked at the ground, shuffled his feet, and wondered if Drew would approve of his choice. "I got a TV for my grandma. Friday was her birthday."

Churches are often asked to give money to the poor, both on an individual basis and a group basis. In poverty, people give disproportionately to the church because Jesus is their friend—not because of stewardship.

In middle class, decision making around money centers on three things: achievement, work, and material security. Things tend to be possessions and the rule about money is this: I don't ask you for money, and you don't ask me.

In wealth, decision making centers around social, financial, and political connections because they keep you safe and help you make more money. Possessions tend to be one-of-a-kind art objects, legacies, and bloodlines. The rule about money is this: You don't talk about it.

But in generational poverty, decision making centers around relationships, entertainment, and survival. People are possessions. And the rule about money and things is this: If you ask me for money and I have it, I need to share it with you.

HOW DOES THIS AFFECT CHURCHES?

The generational poor:

- Tend not to have checking accounts. Financial institutions are distrusted.

- Tend not to support causes in which there is no personal relationship.

- Do not understand church budgets and the need to account for money.

- Sometimes come to church to request money.

- Tend not to plan their own budgets, which often causes the crises they find themselves in.

WHAT CAN CHURCHES DO?

- Provide a repository for savings. Often to save money in poverty, individuals give money to a responsible friend. If anyone asks, they can say, "I don't have any."

- Teach them how to plan backwards (begin with the end in mind).

- Use an envelope system for keeping track of money. (Envelopes are designated for rent, food, etc. Cash is kept in the envelopes.)

OBSERVATION

Many church buildings in the Southern U.S. were just simple wood construction before World War II. The flood of federal money during and after the war (oil, military bases, military manufacturing, etc.) brought to the region a wealth unknown before. Church buildings have shown this affluence by being upgraded to brick or even stone. They are also now almost all air-conditioned. Before the war anyone in the neighborhood could know a great deal about what was going on inside without ever crossing the threshold. The windows were open. From the street you could hear preaching and singing. Now, with our nicer buildings, who could know what's going on inside without entering during a service? In a situation like this, our hospitality becomes crucial!

QUESTIONS

1. We spend money keeping up houses, cars, and other things. How much do you spend guarding your things? How much money do you spend to take care of your money?

2. Who has helped you make financial decisions?

3. How often have you counted on financial help from family or friends to make apparently necessary purchases?

4. How has "who you know" affected your job? The raising of your children?

5. How much would it cost to keep an acceptable wardrobe for your church's gatherings?

6. How much is money a determining factor in choosing (formally or informally) church leaders?

7. What do you mean when you use the phrase, "I just can't afford that"?

SCRIPTURES/ECCLESIASTICUS

*Those who mock the poor insult their Maker; those who are glad at calamity
will not go unpunished.*

– Proverbs 17:5

*Every creature loves its like, and every person the neighbor. All living beings
associate with their own kind, and people stick close to those like themselves.
What does a wolf have in common with a lamb? No more has a sinner with
the devout. What peace is there between a hyena and a dog? And what peace
between the rich and the poor? Wild asses in the wilderness are the prey of lions;
likewise the poor are feeding grounds for the rich. Humility is an abomination
to the proud; likewise the poor are an abomination to the rich.*

– Ecclesiasticus 13:15–20

*My brothers and sisters, do you with your acts of favoritism really believe in our
glorious Lord Jesus Christ? For if a person with gold rings and in fine clothes
comes into your assembly, and if a poor person in dirty clothes also comes in, and
if you take notice of the one wearing the fine clothes and say, "Have a seat here,
please," while to the one who is poor you say, "Stand there," or, "Sit at my feet,"
have you not made distinctions among yourselves, and become judges with evil
thoughts? Listen, my beloved brothers and sisters. Has not God chosen the poor in
the world to be rich in faith and to be heirs of the kingdom that he has promised
to those who love him? But you have dishonored the poor. Is it not the rich who
oppress you? Is it not they who drag you into court? Is it not they who blaspheme
the excellent name that was invoked over you?*

– James 2:1–7

*But when Cephas came to Antioch, I opposed him to his face, because he stood
self-condemned; for until certain people came from James, he used to eat with
the Gentiles. But after they came, he drew back and kept himself separate for
fear of the circumcision faction. And the other Jews joined him in this hypocrisy,
so that even Barnabas was led astray by their hypocrisy.*

– Galatians 2:11–13

{ CHAPTER 7 }

Church Participation

A Story

Jesse walked right off the highway and into the church parking lot. It was full of cars and almost empty of people. He decided to attend the service. There would not be many rides for the next couple of hours. And besides, the morning was getting hot. Jesse followed two people to the main entrance. He wasn't far behind them, but no one held the door. He opened it himself and walked in. The room was much darker than the late-morning sunlight, and it took a minute to be able to see. He heard the music. The service must have already begun. He set his backpack in a corner and followed the sound into the sanctuary.

Jesse found a seat on an outside aisle. He didn't have to ask for room. The couple took one look at him and scooted way down the pew. He nodded thanks to them. It was good he did. They had just given him most of the attention he would get during his visit. The first song was followed by another. Jesse picked up the clean book and considered the words. They were Christian-sounding, but Jesse didn't catch much of their meaning. He didn't sing either. That seemed to be OK. Not many others were singing, at least not very loudly. The organ carried them all.

The sermon was about the prodigal son. It was an uncomfortable lesson for Jesse; contact with his family was none too good. He wasn't sure how the others felt about the sermon. The couple beside him were concentrating on the preaching. (Or were they just intentionally ignoring him?) Otherwise, the people didn't seem too interested. By the time the sermon neared its end,

Jesse wasn't certain that even the preacher was all that excited about what he was saying.

The seat was comfortable, and Jesse had almost fallen asleep. Then the music began again, and quickly everyone stood and began to file out. Jesse shook hands with the minister and asked the question that had been on his mind since he had arrived. "Where's the restroom?" The minister hadn't expected this. Jesse had to ask him twice before he understood.

All things considered, the service was a failure for Jesse and the church. The members had done as much as they could not to notice him, and, although he had seen and heard a lot, Jesse had missed most of what they had hoped he would see.

In poverty, church participation often is on a sporadic basis. Churches in poor neighborhoods usually are led by individuals who have little or no formal training in the ministry but who do have charismatic personalities. Folks in these churches often distrust formal education, rely on the personality of the preacher to keep "the flock" together, depend totally on the preacher's interpretation of the scriptures, require a heavy amount of giving, and are very emotional in approach. They tend to have very few men as members. Often in these churches women are counseled to pray for the men but to stick by their side. Women are not encouraged to take overt action to address problems (alcoholism, infidelity, etc.) but rather to pray for the man's soul and "let God take care of the problem."

In generational poverty, to attend church is to be less than a man. As noted in the last question of Chapter Five, what does church have to offer a fighter and a lover? At times a man will let his wife attend if it isn't interfering in daily life. But if the wife gets too attached to the church or the people in the church, then the husband likely will put up some diversionary roadblocks (he may demand that she be there to cook him breakfast, he may get drunk so that she will have to rescue him, he may make life very difficult, he may refuse to give her money, he may refuse to drive her to church, etc.).

However, if his perception is that the wife and children are happy and his life is going fairly smoothly, he will sometimes give his blessing and look forward to the quiet time at home when they're all away at church.

OBSERVATION
What We Don't See

Although Christianity puts itself forward as primarily a spiritual society, it is not the spiritual side that is first encountered.

Christians who meet regularly know who they are and why they come together. Their services, no matter how elaborate or meaningful, become normal after a time, and they know from moment to moment what to expect. This can be deceiving. The forms their gatherings take—a certain building and time, particular words, music and actions—these are not the true essence of their coming together. Rather, the forms are there to help the members contact the Deity or to remind them of spiritual truth.

The irony is that for the visitor the words and actions of the church always happen amidst a backdrop of the incidental and accidental. No matter how hard church members try, they will still display more of themselves— their true priorities and weaknesses—than they mean to show. The color of the carpet may have been chosen last decade. Most of the music was written in another age. The minister and all those gathered will have their good and average Sundays. The visitor will sense all that is there without the benefit of protocol. He/she is like the child who saw the emperor's "new clothes" for all that they were not.

QUESTIONS

1. If someone with real need (spiritual, physical, or social) visited your church, what opportunity would they have to express that need? What hope would they have of the need being met? If they could not express the need, what would be offered to them otherwise?

2. It's not uncommon for there to be a large list of unspoken rules of conduct at a given church gathering. What kinds of responses could be expected when someone breaks these rules? (Perhaps a child cries or misbehaves; someone might interrupt a speaker with a question; subjects of conversation or just questions that usually aren't raised are brought up; etc.) How might a church gathering be designed to be more open?

3. If the usual gatherings of your church could not easily accommodate unusual behavior, could another time or place better meet this need?

SCRIPTURES/ECCLESIASTICUS

Do not withhold good from those to whom it is due, when it is in your power to do it. Do not say to your neighbor, "Go, and come again, tomorrow I will give it"—when you have it with you.

– Proverbs 3:27–28

Nevertheless, be patient with someone in humble circumstances, and do not keep him waiting for your alms.

– Ecclesiasticus 29:8

What good is it, my brothers and sisters, if you say you have faith but do not have works? Can faith save you? If a brother or sister is naked and lacks daily food, and one of you says to them, "Go in peace; keep warm and eat your fill," and yet you do not supply their bodily needs, what is the good of that? So faith by itself, if it has no works, is dead.

– James 2:14–17

CHAPTER 8

Whom Do We Help and How Much?

A Story

Bonnie didn't mean for it to turn out this way. She had seen David on the street for years. He was a young man, some of whose needs were obvious enough. On any given day he might be here or there in town, riding on his bicycle, collecting aluminum cans, or "just there." Bonnie had lived with the slight discomfort of seeing him and doing nothing to touch his life for a long time. But then came that sermon!

The next time she saw him she stopped and talked with him. She also invited him to come to church with her. His response of surprise and excitement had delighted her.

That first Sunday she picked him up at the corner. There were awkward moments, but all in all the morning went well. It was even fun to introduce David to those around. This was what it was all about: bringing another person closer to the Kingdom of God.

The next week she picked him up again. He now knew some of the routine of the service. He seemed to love to watch the young children. But there was one problem. It didn't matter to whom he was introduced, he stayed with her. The word "shadow" came to her mind. By the third week Bonnie began to feel the loss of contact with her friends. They hardly knew how to deal with David, so they kept their distance. Bonnie missed keeping up on all the news. One thing was clear. Though she wanted David to connect with the church, he remained her responsibility. He was not the church's guest. He was her guest.

As the weeks went by, it became harder and harder to stop and pick him up.

One of the issues many churches face is: Do we help this person or not? And then the question often becomes: How much help do we give him/her?

One of the first things to remember is that mutual respect can be difficult if not impossible to maintain when one person is always the giver and the other person is always the receiver.

A second guideline is usually to not give cash (see further discussion on page 118). The reason is that if the relationship is complicated by a situation that has destructive or addictive patterns, the cash will seldom go for what was requested.

A third guideline is that many tangibles (clothes, furniture, etc.) are often sold for cash to purchase other items.

A fourth guideline is to analyze the resources of the individual seeking— or simply needing—assistance.

RESOURCES

Typically, poverty is thought of in terms of financial resources only. However, the reality is that *financial resources,* while extremely important, do not explain the differences in the success with which individuals leave poverty nor the reasons that many stay in poverty. The ability to leave poverty is more dependent upon other resources than it is upon financial resources. Each of these resources plays a vital role in the success of an individual.

Emotional resources provide the stamina to withstand difficult and uncomfortable emotional situations and feelings. Emotional resources are the most important of all resources because, when present, they allow the individual not to return to old habit patterns. In order to move from poverty to middle class or middle class to wealth, an individual must suspend his/her "emotional memory bank" because the situations and hidden rules are so unlike what he/she has experienced previously. Therefore, a certain level of persistence and an ability to stay with the situation until it can be learned

Types of Resources

FINANCIAL: Having the money to purchase goods and services.

EMOTIONAL: Being able to choose and control emotional responses, particularly to negative situations, without engaging in self-destructive behavior. This is an internal resource and shows itself through stamina, perseverance, and choices.

MENTAL: Having the mental abilities and acquired skills (reading, writing, computing) to deal with daily life.

SPIRITUAL: Believing in divine purpose and guidance.

PHYSICAL: Having physical health and mobility.

SUPPORT SYSTEMS: Having friends, family, and backup resources available to access in times of need. These are external resources.

RELATIONSHIPS/ROLE MODELS: Having frequent access to adult(s) who are appropriate, who are *nurturing* to the child, and who do not engage in self-destructive behavior.

KNOWLEDGE OF HIDDEN RULES: Knowing the unspoken cues and habits of a group.

(and therefore feel comfortable) are necessary. This persistence (i.e., staying with the situation) is proof that emotional resources are present. Emotional resources come, at least in part, from role models.

Mental resources are simply being able to process information and use it in daily living. If an individual can read, write, and compute, he/she has a decided advantage. That person can access information from many different free sources, as well as be somewhat self-sufficient.

Spiritual resources are the belief that help can be obtained from a higher power, that there is a purpose for living, and that worth and love are gifts from God. This is a powerful resource because the individual does not see himself/herself as hopeless and useless, but rather as capable and having worth and value.

Physical resources are having a body that works, that is capable and mobile. The individual can be self-sufficient.

A *support system* is a resource. To whom does one go when help is needed? Those individuals available and who will help are resources. When the child is sick and you have to be at work—who takes care of the child? Where do you go when money is short and the baby needs medicine? Support systems are not just about meeting financial or emotional needs. They are about knowledge bases as well. How do you get into college? Who sits and listens when you get rejected? Who helps you negotiate the mountains of paper? Who assists you with your algebra homework when you don't know how to do it? Those people are all support systems.

Relationships/role models are resources. All individuals have role models. The question is the extent to which the role model is nurturing or appropriate. Can the role model parent? Work successfully? Provide a gender role for the individual? It is largely from role models that the person learns how to live life emotionally.

Knowledge of hidden rules is crucial to whatever class in which the individual wishes to live. Hidden rules exist in poverty, in middle class, and in wealth, as well as in ethnic groups and other units of people. Hidden rules are about the salient, unspoken understandings that cue the members of the group that this individual does or does not fit. For example, three of the hidden rules in poverty are the following: The noise level is high (the TV is almost always on and everyone may talk at once), the most important information is non-verbal, and one of the main values of an individual to the group is an ability to entertain. There are hidden rules about food, dress, decorum, etc. Generally, in order to successfully move from one class to the next, it is important to have a spouse or mentor from the class to which you wish to move to model and teach you the hidden rules.

SCRIPTURES

Financial

The wealth of the rich is their fortress; the poverty of the poor is their ruin.

– Proverbs 10:15

Emotional

Fools show their anger at once, but the prudent ignore an insult.

– Proverbs 12:16

One who is slow to anger is better than the mighty, and one whose temper is controlled than one who captures a city.

– Proverbs 16:32

Mental

By wisdom a house is built, and by understanding it is established; by knowledge the rooms are filled with all precious and pleasant riches. Wise warriors are mightier than strong ones, and those who have knowledge than those who have strength; for by wise guidance you can wage your war, and in abundance of counselors there is victory.

– Proverbs 24:3–6

Spiritual

The reward for humility and fear of the LORD is riches and honor and life.

– Proverbs 22:4

Physical

The glory of youths is their strength, but the beauty of the aged is their gray hair.

– Proverbs 20:29

Support Systems

Some friends play at friendship but a true friend sticks closer than one's nearest kin.

– Proverbs 18:24

Relationships/Role Models

The teaching of the wise is a fountain of life, so that one may avoid the snares of death.

– Proverbs 13:14

Knowledge of Hidden Rules

When you sit down to eat with a ruler, observe carefully what is before you, and put a knife to your throat if you have a big appetite. Do not desire the ruler's delicacies, for they are deceptive food.

– Proverbs 23:1–3

OBSERVATION

Three significant needs stand at the forefront when individuals come to a church for help. The needs have to do with money, friends, and spiritual strength. That's generally the order of occurrence at the church door. A multitude come for financial help, a smaller number ask for friendship, and only a few openly express spiritual need.

Churches, in turn, openly offer help in the same three areas, but usually hoping for people to come with needs in the opposite order: first, spiritual strength; second, friendship; and last, money. That people do not come this way is disconcerting. But much more difficult is the degree of needs that they bring. A little money, friendship, or spiritual consolation is not so hard to give. When huge amounts are needed, it is a wholly different matter.

Friendship would seem to be the easiest of the three to give. It is not always so.

QUESTIONS

1. Of eight resources (financial, emotional, mental, spiritual, physical, support systems, relationships/role models, and knowledge of hidden rules), which ones does your church give the most help with? Which the least? At which resources should the church excel?

2. Which of the resources can be offered quickly? Which take longer?

3. Share some of the better experiences you have had trying to help someone. What do these experiences have in common?

4. Where do you want those you have helped to be (physically, socially, spiritually) after you have helped them? How long is it likely to take them to get there?

SCRIPTURES/ECCLESIASTICUS

*Speak out for those who cannot speak, for the rights of all the destitute.
Speak out, judge righteously, defend the rights of the poor and needy.*

– Proverbs 31:8–9

*Endear yourself to the congregation; bow your head low to the great. Give a
hearing to the poor, and return their greeting politely. Rescue the oppressed
from the oppressor; and do not be hesitant in giving a verdict. Be a father to
orphans, and be like a husband to their mother; you will then be like a son
of the Most High, and he will love you more than does your mother.*

– Ecclesiasticus 4:7–10

*Consider your own call, brothers and sisters: not many of you were wise by
human standards, not many were powerful, not many were of noble birth.
But God chose what is foolish in the world to shame the wise; God chose
what is weak in the world to shame the strong; God chose what is low
and despised in the world, things that are not, to reduce to nothing things
that are, so that no one might boast in the presence of God. He is the source
of your life in Christ Jesus, who became for us wisdom from God, and
righteousness and sanctification and redemption, in order that, as it is
written, "Let the one who boasts, boast in the Lord."*

– 1 Corinthians 1:26–31

CHAPTER 9

Transitioning the Poor into Membership

A Story

Tammy and Heather first began attending the church when their mother was invited by her employer. Through the years the girls became part of the crowd. Their clothes were not so nice or varied as the other children's, but for a while few had noticed or cared. Tammy and Heather made friends with the children of other members. They visited in the other kids' homes, though not many came to their house.

Tammy and Heather's blossoming into puberty was no less than the other girls', just less decorated by current trends. About this time, their standing among the church's children changed. They were not invited into the world of adolescence and dating in the same way as their friends. A few of the boys showed Tammy and Heather some attention—at times appropriate, more often inappropriate—but even this happened less and less. There were some dates, but never in the context of the nicer events. Tammy and Heather, who had at one time felt like full members, knew that something was no longer the same. They came less and less and then disappeared.

Another issue for many churches is how to "transition" the poor into membership, because often they will not attend the church services as they are currently structured. Individuals in poverty often do not understand formal register, find middle-class services stilted and boring, and consider the music lifeless and unemotional. Further, the church members complain about the behavior of the new children in church and Sunday school.

SUGGESTIONS

- Have two separate services. Have the traditional one at the regular time. Put in a second service that is close to lunch, is very informal, and follows with a meal. To participate in the meal, each person has to bring something. That way mutual respect can be built. The regular members who wish to participate in this ministry may come. Those who don't wish to participate simply don't return for the noon meal.

- Teach appropriate social skills and behavior to the children as part of Sunday school. It isn't realistic to expect that new children will instantly know the rules. There is no one to teach them. Do not single students out for individual praise. This often alienates other students. Don't have favorite students either. Rather, practice the skills as a group. Give food as a reward for appropriate behavior (e.g., "When you begin your drawing, I'll give you a Jolly Rogers® candy").

- Make sure that Sunday school is full of Bible stories, participatory music (clapping, etc.), and art/coloring activities. Also allow for some movement. Have a snack in Sunday school. Other activities that work are acting out Bible stories and videotaping them, putting murals of the stories on butcher-block paper, and (for older students) adapting Bible stories to modern-day life through role playing. If students throw comments into the story while it's being told, allow that to happen the first couple of times.

- The memorization of Bible verses to rhythm patterns or music as a kind of choral response is also valuable. Individual memorization and recitation are not always well-received. It works better as a paired or group activity.

■ Remember that transition into church membership often is characterized by a period of "in and out." They come for a while, then they don't come for a while. Accept this as part of the transition. Also know that some will not return, while others eventually will become members.

OBSERVATIONS

There was a time when a church building could have a more open role in the separation of social groups. Monuments in the building to this or that individual were placed where they could display the significance of the donor family. Some pews were designated for the exclusive use of a family. Position and distance were thereby maintained. The church in such a case would help keep proper order and uphold status, even if that church building was the only one in town.

Today such distance and position have been preserved by multiple buildings and fellowships. Members of a congregation can buy a building located in a place convenient to their group. It's only fair to mention that a location might be chosen because of its inconvenience to certain other groups. Some churches have thereby developed a strategy for excluding less desired elements. The people they don't want don't live nearby, or at least they're not openly invited.

But what if some individuals from one of those groups were invited or just came? What if a family or two from the poor broke through all the barriers . . . and brought their children?!

Churches are volunteer organizations. As a rule, individuals come to a church because they find something there that they want. The exception of required attendance is usually the result of the efforts of a forceful parent or grandparent.

One of the most popular reasons to take part in a church is association. People want connections with people. Friendships found within the fellowship of a church may not always be easily acquired, but once made, they can be very good indeed. People need a sense of forgiveness/love from God and a sense of connection with people.

New families often are welcomed according to two basic traits: Is the couple good-looking? And is the couple outgoing? Failing these, a family too often is left to its own devices to connect with the congregation.

Most "baby boomers" have heard of the traveling hobos who would come to homes looking for a meal. With these stories have come the rumors of marks left on curbs or porches that told which homes would help. Nothing in our years can confirm or deny such marks.

We suspect that some of the marks the hobos observed were of another sort altogether. What makes a home look hospitable to strangers? It might be a yard worn by lots of children or visitors. Perhaps porch furniture not too neatly placed, or a door heavily used. Maybe the welcome mat was dirtier than that of the other homes.

We wonder what would make a church look hospitable to those who call with need.

Individuals move upward (classwise) generally at the expense of relationships. It is a stunning point, especially in the context of middle-class Christianity. Amazingly, the church tends to offer new relationships only at the cost of old ones. "If any want to become my followers, let them deny themselves and take up their cross daily and follow me" (Luke 9:23).

QUESTIONS

1. What things qualify someone for leadership in your church? Money? Connections? Formal education? Intelligence? Stability? Spirituality?

2. How open are the members of your church to the inclusion of different people?

3. What are the taboos at one of your church's gatherings? Particular clothing (e.g., skirt length)? Noise level of conversation (e.g., appropriate ways of greeting)? Expressions of need (e.g., "I need money")?

SCRIPTURES

He said also to the one who had invited him, "When you give a luncheon or a dinner, do not invite your friends or your brothers or your relatives or rich neighbors, in case they may invite you in return, and you would be repaid. But when you give a banquet, invite the poor, the crippled, the lame, and the blind. And you will be blessed, because they cannot repay you, for you will be repaid at the resurrection of the righteous." One of the dinner guests, on hearing this, said to him, "Blessed is anyone who will eat bread in the kingdom of God!" Then Jesus said to him, "Someone gave a great dinner and invited many. At the time for the dinner he sent his slave to say to those who had been invited, 'Come; for everything is ready now.' But they all alike began to make excuses. The first said to him, 'I have bought a piece of land, and I must go out and see it; please accept my regrets.' Another said, 'I have bought five yoke of oxen, and I am going to try them out; please accept my regrets.' Another said, 'I have just been married, and therefore I cannot come.' So the slave returned and reported this to his master. Then the owner of the house became angry and said to his slave, 'Go out at once into the streets and lanes of the town and bring in the poor, the crippled, the blind, and the lame.' And the slave said, 'Sir, what you ordered has been done, and there is still room.' Then the master said to the slave, 'Go out into the roads and lanes, and compel people to come in, so that my house may be filled. For I tell you, none of those who were invited will taste my dinner.' "

– Luke 14:12–24

When he had come to Jerusalem, he attempted to join the disciples; and they were all afraid of him, for they did not believe that he was a disciple. But Barnabas took him, brought him to the apostles, and described for them how on the road he had seen the Lord, who had spoken to him, and how in Damascus he had spoken boldly in the name of Jesus.

– Acts 9:26–27

{ CHAPTER 10 }

Issues with Integrating the Poor into the Church

A Story

I was invited into the trailer. It was before school was out, but the children were home. There were three of them, all freshly washed. The mother welcomed me to take a seat on a cluttered couch. Without asking, I was given the reason for the children being out of school. They had been sent home because of head lice. It was somewhat difficult to make myself comfortable.

A Story

Debbie came back to church. It had been 15 years since she and her family had stopped attending. A serious illness and an old friend had encouraged her. But she did not come alone. She dragged along two sisters, an assortment of in-laws, and a troupe of their children and stepchildren. The total came to more than 20! Most of them were new to the church scene. Some of them brought along their own sense of morality and legality.

Their arrival was a bit of a shock to all concerned. The church was ready to handle new arrivals one family at a time. Debbie brought four or five. The church preferred to acculturate new members. Debbie had brought her own peer group!

For Debbie, the shock was just as real. She had imagined the church just as she had left it. Now, few of the faces were the same. More significantly, some of the things she had counted on were not there. The preacher Debbie remembered would have straightened out Scott, her husband. And the old dinners they used to have out on the lawn may have been under sweltering conditions, but they were one of her favorite memories. These people were nice, but they just didn't feel like home.

A Story

Sarah liked the folks at her church. They were good people and seemed to care. She and her children didn't take part fully in the lives of many in the congregation, but the members did welcome her into their conversations. They also brought her many things. Often they gave clothes—used, of course, but nicer than she had. And if they weren't all useful, many of them were. And even if some of the gifts seemed a bit impersonal, it wasn't too hard to smile and accept them anyway.

Advice was pretty common too. Less of this was as useful. "You should get a computer." "You should get a newer car." (Out of the question—no money.) "Get the boys out mowing yards this summer." (They had always lived in apartments. Neither of them had ever touched a lawnmower.) "You should see a doctor about that." (The county hospital was always a day lost to work and pay.) Few of those who gave such recommendations stayed around for any of her thoughts. In the end, there seemed little point in explaining why she hadn't tried many of their ideas.

The truth was that the church knew little of her world. And when she brought someone from her neighborhood, her guest was largely ignored.

(It isn't hard to have one poor family in a church. The second, third, et al. . . . those are the tougher ones.)

A Story

Bill and his family came into the sanctuary and sat in their usual place. It was a comfortable feeling, being there together. The family took up most of a pew. Years ago, when Bill and his wife had first moved to the area and joined the congregation, they were only a family of four. Many years had passed since then. Two more children came, and then all those years of raising the kids. Now three of their children had their own spouses, and there were two grandkids! They were all healthy and doing well. Bill couldn't help but feel a sense of pride and, almost equally, a belief that he and his wife had been truly blessed.

As the seats filled, it was clear that there would be a good crowd today. Another blessing! People were coming. The congregation was doing well.

Then in came that family again. Bill imagined that they were from the apartments nearby. "What are they doing here anyway? Their car is about to fall apart. Most of the time the father doesn't come. When he does, he just frowns through most of the service and ignores his own kids' misbehavior. Doris says that one of their kids has been picking on one of the grandkids at school! Why don't they find a church full of people like themselves? Why are they coming back this far to find a seat?!" "Oh, yeah, the seats were filling up at the front." It would be hard to hear the sermon today. That family was just such a distraction.

Bill wasn't happy for the rest of the service. He knew all about that "loving others" stuff; he just hadn't planned on doing it in a church service when he needed to tend to his own family. "Why do families like that have to be *my* problem?" The truth was that such people were not the reason he and his family had joined that church in the first place. It just wasn't the same church anymore.

The key to membership for individuals from poverty is in creating relationships with them. Because poverty is about relationships *and* entertainment, the most significant motivator for these individuals is relationships.

The question becomes, How does a formal institution create relationships? Two sources provide some answers to this question. These sources are (1) the recent research in the field of science and (2) the work Stephen Covey has done with personal effectiveness.

Margaret Wheatley, in her book *Leadership and the New Science* (1992), states quite clearly:

> *Scientists in many different disciplines are questioning whether we can adequately explain how the world works by using the machine imagery created in the 17th century, most notably by Sir Isaac Newton. In the machine model, one must understand parts. Things can be taken apart, dissected literally or representationally . . . and then put back together without any significant loss . . . The Newtonian model of the world is characterized by materialism and reductionism—a focus on things rather than relationships . . . The quantum view of reality strikes against most of our notions of reality. Even to scientists, it is admittedly bizarre. But it is a world where* relationship *is the key determiner of what is observed and of how particles manifest themselves . . . Many scientists now work with the concept of fields—invisible forces that structure space or behavior* (pp. 8–13).

Wheatley goes on to say that, in the new science of quantum physics, physical reality is not just tangible, it is also intangible. Fields are invisible, yet:

> *[They are the] substance of the universe . . . In organizations, which is the more important influence on behavior—the system or the individual? The quantum world answered that question: It depends . . . What is critical is the relationship created between the person and the setting. That relationship will always be different, will always evoke different potentialities. It all* depends on the players and the moment (pp. 34–35).

Both ministers and the laity have always known that relationships, often referred to as "politics," make a great deal of difference—sometimes all the difference—in what could or could not happen in church life. The most important part of personal growth seems related to relationships, if we listen to the data and the potent realities in the research emerging from the disciplines of biology and physics.

When individuals who have been in poverty (and have successfully made it into middle class) are asked how they made the journey, the answer nine times out of ten has to do with a relationship—a person who made a suggestion or took an interest in them as individuals.

Stephen Covey (1989) uses the notion of an emotional bank account to convey the crucial aspects of relationships. He indicates that in all relationships one makes deposits to and withdrawals from the other individual in that relationship. In his view, the following are the deposits and withdrawals:

DEPOSITS	WITHDRAWALS
Seek first to understand	Seek first to be understood
Keeping promises	Breaking promises
Kindnesses, courtesies	Unkindnesses, discourtesies
Clarifying expectations	Violating expectations
Loyalty to the absent	Disloyalty, duplicity
Apologies	Pride, conceit, arrogance
Open to feedback	Rejecting feedback

Adapted from Stephen Covey, *The Seven Habits of Highly Effective People*

The first step in creating relationships with adults is to make the deposits that are the basis of relationships. Relationships usually begin as one individual to another.

What are the deposits and withdrawals with regard to individuals from poverty? (See chart on next page.) By understanding deposits that are valued by individuals from poverty, the relationship is stronger.

DEPOSITS MADE TO INDIVIDUAL IN POVERTY	WITHDRAWALS MADE FROM INDIVIDUAL IN POVERTY
Appreciation for humor and entertainment provided by the individual	Put-downs or sarcasm about the humor or the individual
Acceptance of what the individual cannot say about a person or situation	Insistence and demands for full explanation about a person or situation
Respect for the demands and priorities of relationships	Insistence on the middle-class view of relationships
Using the adult voice	Using the parent voice
Assisting with goal-setting	Telling the individual his/her goals
Identifying options related to available resources	Making judgments on the value and availability of resources
Understanding the importance of personal freedom, speech, and individual personality	Assigning pejorative character traits to the individual

How does a congregation create—and build—relationships? Through support systems, through caring about individuals, by promoting individual achievement, by being role models, by insisting upon successful behaviors in the church setting. *Support systems are simply networks of relationships.*

Will creating healthy relationships make all individuals from poverty successful? No. But if we make a difference for 5% the first year and 5% more each year thereafter, we will have progressed considerably from where we are right now.

In the final analysis, as one looks back, it is the relationships one remembers.

OBSERVATIONS

To make a church seem like home, you need friends, or at least people who help you feel welcome. New faces must either find friends in the congregation or bring their own. Security comes in numbers, and sometimes, so does salvation.

People like to find others like themselves. They understand each other's jokes, concerns, and most of all their rules. Churches will be affected by this. The greater welcome is granted to the ones who arrive and know the setting and the system. Those who don't know these things will not be trusted quickly and will not easily find places to serve.

When the "comfort of commonness" (or familiarity) settles in at a given congregation, the church may begin to represent a single stratum of society. The stratum may not be exactly defined and may develop a certain depth, but it will have boundaries. Children, young adults, couples, and senior members will all be connected by limited social and/or cultural norms and expectations. Those outside the stratum (perhaps economically above or below it) will not connect easily with that church. No matter how hard the church members try to reach out, many visitors and "prospects" will slip through their fingers.

There will be exceptions, to be sure. A poor individual may connect with a more affluent congregation. Even a rich and powerful family may happily mix with a middle-class church. But in either case, one thing is usually true: The connection by the outsider will be made, not because the church knows how to deal with the outsider, but because the outsider knows how to deal with the church.

QUESTIONS

1. What relationships did you lose when you became a Christian?

2. What systems does your congregation have to welcome individuals who do not easily fit in? What systems might it develop?

3. People who have been longtime members of a congregation can develop many ties with one another. Some ties are spiritual, and many are from shared experiences. What are the things you share with members of your church? How important are the spiritual ties among members who are friends?

4. Christianity has a significant social side. Individuals who are longtime members look forward to renewing friendly contacts. A new face, even an economically and socially similar one, can have a difficult time finding a place. The poor are just as interested in social contacts as anyone else. How will members handle the different interests and concerns of the poor?

5. What are the reasons you keep coming back to your church? Friends? Family? Habits? Valuable contacts in the community? Spiritual reasons?

6. Why would someone from the outside want to come to your church?

7. Placing the promise of heaven to the side, what are the effects of becoming a Christian on life now? What might it cost? What might be the benefits?

8. When two people marry, they also are connecting strongly with each other's immediate and extended families (whether they want to or not). New members to a congregation may bring along their families too. How open are your doors to strangers?

SCRIPTURE

I therefore, the prisoner in the Lord, beg you to lead a life worthy of the calling to which you have been called, with all humility and gentleness, with patience, bearing with one another in love, making every effort to maintain the unity of the Spirit in the bond of peace. There is one body and one Spirit, just as you were called to the one hope of your calling, one Lord, one faith, one baptism, one God and Father of all, who is above all and through all and in all. But each of us was given grace according to the measure of Christ's gift. The gifts he gave were that some would be apostles, some prophets, some evangelists, some pastors and teachers, to equip the saints for the work of ministry, for building up the body of Christ, until all of us come to the unity of the faith and of the knowledge of the Son of God, to maturity, to the measure of the full stature of Christ. We must no longer be children, tossed to and fro and blown about by every wind of doctrine, by people's trickery, by their craftiness in deceitful scheming. But speaking the truth in love, we must grow up in every way into him who is the head, into Christ, from whom the whole body, joined and knit together by every ligament with which it is equipped, as each part is working properly, promotes the body's growth in building itself up in love.

– Ephesians 4:1–7, 11–16

SCRIPTURES

"When the Son of Man comes in his glory, and all the angels with him, then he will sit on the throne of his glory. All the nations will be gathered before him, and he will separate people one from another as a shepherd separates the sheep from the goats, and he will put the sheep at his right hand and the goats at the left. Then the king will say to those at his right hand, 'Come, you that are blessed by my Father, inherit the kingdom prepared for you from the foundation of the world; for I was hungry and you gave me food, I was thirsty and you gave me something to drink, I was a stranger and you welcomed me, I was naked and you gave me clothing, I was sick and you took care of me, I was in prison and you visited me.' Then the righteous will answer him, 'Lord, when was it that we saw you hungry and gave you food, or thirsty and gave you something to drink? And when was it that we saw you a stranger and welcomed you, or naked and gave you clothing? And when was it that we saw you sick or in prison and visited you?' And the king will answer them, 'Truly I tell you, just as you did it to one of the least of these who are members of my family, you did it to me.' Then he will say to those at his left hand, 'You that are accursed, depart from me into the eternal fire prepared for the devil and his angels; for I was hungry and you gave me no food, I was thirsty and you gave me nothing to drink, I was a stranger and you did not welcome me, naked and you did not give me clothing, sick and in prison and you did not visit me.' Then they also will answer, 'Lord, when was it that we saw you hungry or thirsty or a stranger or naked or sick or in prison, and did not take care of you?' Then he will answer them, 'Truly I tell you, just as you did not do it to one of the least of these, you did not do it to me.' And these will go away into eternal punishment, but the righteous into eternal life."

— Matthew 25:31–46

And let us consider how to provoke one another to love and good deeds, not neglecting to meet together, as is the habit of some, but encouraging one another, and all the more as you see the Day approaching.

— Hebrews 10:24–25

{ CHAPTER 11 }

Systemic Issues in Church Organizations

A Story

The preacher had arrived at one of those pleasant plateaus in life. His son, though not yet fully independent, was an adult. It was all the more enjoyable that he had arrived without having stepped off into any of the nastier pitfalls of life along the way. One of the greatest delights was that the son would talk. One day, as they discussed the son's future plans, the topic of college came up. The preacher offered the wisdom he had often taught—that a university degree was not the only path to a good life. His son looked him straight in the eye and said, "Right! And just what would it be like in a few years when I showed up at a family reunion without a degree?" The preacher knew that the son spoke truly. A degree was a family standard, no matter what he had preached, no matter what was the truth.

Preachers and Christians say a lot of true things. They also know that to speak truth and to live truth are not always the same thing.

A Story

A minister with a great gift for speaking found himself traveling the U.S. addressing adults and teenagers about their troubles and about Jesus Christ and his church. This brought him into contact with many Christians and churches. He was genuinely respected for how he used his gift of preaching and was regularly asked for advice from individuals and leaders on many topics. As he traveled he was able to see more than most preachers about just how the church was doing. Sometimes he was concerned about what he saw.

He developed two questions that he tried to ask of congregational leaders. The questions helped him see how things were going. He hoped they would also help leaders see ahead. The questions were: (1) Do you have a plan to help your church grow? (2) If your congregation were to suddenly double or triple in size, do you know how you would handle all the new faces and the changes they would bring to you?

The minister said that only one of the many congregations said yes to the first question. Not one had any answers for the second. That was more than 20 years ago. The difficulties of churches seem to have grown in that time. The second question remains haunting. What if they came?

For large church organizations, systemic issues affect the ability of particular congregations to make interventions with individuals from poverty.

First of all, to be viable, church organizations must maintain an economic base. This comes through membership. Because church membership is voluntary, the church must offer the services that the paying membership finds valuable. This often creates a conflict with the ministry to individuals in poverty. Ministers who feel this calling to work with the poor are sometimes alienated from the congregation and asked to leave. A minister is valuable if he or she "grows" the church (i.e., increases membership and giving). Church organizations compound the problem in a systemic way as well through the data that are collected. If the larger organization asks only for data about membership and giving, then the value of a minister is based on those factors. But if the organization also asks the following ten questions, two things happen: (1) The church organization builds an economic basis for the future, and (2) the church keeps its current economic base.

Sample Kinds of Questions

1. How many interventions were made in neighborhoods of poverty?

2. What kinds and how many linkages were established with social service agencies?

3. How many one-on-one relationships were established with individuals from poverty?

4. How many new faces were in your congregation in the past year?

5. How many individuals were helped with the transition from poverty to work?

6. What kinds of continuing education did the church provide to assist with transition?

7. What anecdotal records were collected from visitors to the church?

8. What kinds of problems and resistance were encountered from the current membership? From those contemplating membership?

9. What is the congregation's long-range plan for working with the poor?

10. What specific interventions were made in educating mothers in poverty?

In the mid-1990s one of the major church denominations in America did an in-depth demographic survey and found that the majority of growth would be in inner cities and suburbs among the situationally and generationally poor. In addition, they found that the membership (in the transitioning areas from middle class to poverty) was dropping. The individuals who were staying in these neighborhoods were older; in 20 years they would no longer be able to give to the church but instead would expect support and assistance from the church. The researchers also found that a move to the new and growing suburbs had two problems: (1) To replace the quality and size of the current facilities was cost-prohibitive and (2) the new membership, which was younger, simply does not give the way the older membership does. Therefore, this denomination made a conscious effort to begin building inner-city membership among the poor—knowing that it will not pay off for 20 years. But they know that their economic base will stabilize over time.

HOW DOES A CHURCH BEGIN A SYSTEMIC EFFORT TO BUILD A CONGREGATION INVOLVING MANY PEOPLE WHO LIVE IN POVERTY?

1. Collect a wider database about activities based on current needs and the development needed for the future.

2. Have a two-pronged approach to long-term development. Prong 1 is immediate intervention into preventing the development of the fighter/lover identity in males and immediate intervention into enhancing the education of mothers. Prong 2 is promoting an increase in education for young females. The highest correlation with the level of education a child reaches is the level of education of the mother. As long as mothers in poverty are uneducated, they will often have men in and out of the house to help with financial support. This role-modeling greatly enhances the tendency for male identity to be a fighter and a lover. The two highest correlations with poverty are family structure and level of educational attainment.

3. Incorporate into the ministry with the poor the notion of mutual respect. In other words, almost all of a church's interventions require some form of reciprocal participation on the part of the individual from poverty. As noted earlier, there can be no long-term mutual respect when one person is always the giver and the other is always the taker.

4. Identify and establish "mission churches" in poor neighborhoods. Find ministers who enjoy working with the poor. Keep those ministers in those positions for at least ten years to establish relationships and stability.

OBSERVATIONS

Another view of the value of considering the church's care of the poor: Christianity, of course, is far bigger than the United States. What Christians do to help others will have ramifications far beyond our borders and our time. Our failure to connect with the poor could have hard results. There is no doubt that Islam sees "fields ready for harvest" in the inner cities, which Christianity has all but vacated. Not all are troubled by this. Still the Lord who said, "Just as you did not [help] one of the least of these, you did not [help] me" (Matthew 25:45) may find our indifference to the poor a failing beyond his mercy.

It would be vain to think that everything was up to us, but most Christians believe that somehow, mysteriously and paradoxically, each of us takes part in the dispensing of God's goodness on earth. That there are problems presented in the poverty we find around us is conceded by most of us. The extended affluence since World War II set us up for the painful surprises of the poverty of our cities. The flight of churches from inner cities has only exacerbated the difficulties. Many Christians are not only too far away from the problems to help, they are also too far to easily understand what is going on. Still, such problems are what faith is for. Christianity promises power beyond us and affords us hope beyond our abilities. We might take solace in the words of Paul (Philippians 2:5–7a), "Let the same mind be in you that was in Christ Jesus, who, though he was in the form of God, did not regard equality with God as something to be exploited, but emptied himself, taking the form of a slave, . . ." He must have thought we could do just that! And so we begin.

We might also reflect on James 2:5: "Listen, my beloved brothers and sisters: Has not God chosen the poor in the world to be rich in faith and to be heirs of the kingdom that he has promised to those who love him?"

It must be acknowledged that there is truth to statements like "But that won't work" and "We tried that, and it didn't work." Many things are indeed doomed to failure from their inception. However, these observations take only limited thought (they are usually among the first excuses for inactivity) and less heart. Many of the troubles the church faces may not "technically" be new, but they are surely new to most of our generation. If we are to address the problems of the people around us, we will need both our hearts and our heads. Success will not often lie with those who only see the failures ahead. More often it will be with those who strain their vision to see what might work and who have the courage to try.

QUESTIONS

1. It may seem a long time, but it hasn't yet been a lifetime since segregation. How many of your current leaders never attended integrated schools?

2. How far do your members travel to attend services? How far did members travel 30 years ago?

3. With many more people traveling greater distances to work and more wives working away from home, there has come a loss of discretionary time. How has meal preparation changed from the days of your parents? When is housework done? How have volunteer hours been affected at your church? [Not everyone believes that time has so greatly changed. After studying this carefully for eight years, I know it has greatly affected the lives of church members in my community. It's not unusual for individuals to have lost 10% of their discretionary time traveling to and from work!]

4. Who among your congregation's membership lives within one mile of your building? Five miles? What about the last congregation you attended?

5. What do you know about the needs and concerns of those who live near your building?

6. Is a language other than English spoken by large numbers in your community? Who among our members speaks this language fluently?

SCRIPTURES/ECCLESIASTICUS

Since there will never cease to be some in need on the earth, I therefore command you, "Open your hand to the poor and needy neighbor in your land."

— Deuteronomy 15:11

This was the guilt of your sister Sodom: she and her daughters had pride, excess of food, and prosperous ease, but did not aid the poor and needy.

— Ezekiel 16:49

Now during those days, when the disciples were increasing in number, the Hellenists complained against the Hebrews because their widows were being neglected in the daily distribution of food. And the twelve called together the whole community of the disciples and said, "It is not right that we should neglect the word of God in order to wait on tables. Therefore, friends, select from among yourselves seven men of good standing, full of the Spirit and of wisdom, whom we may appoint to this task, while we, for our part, will devote ourselves to prayer and to serving the word." What they said pleased the whole community, and they chose Stephen, a man full of faith and the Holy Spirit, together with Philip, Prochorus, Nicanor, Timon, Parmenas, and Nicolaus, a proselyte of Antioch. They had these men stand before the apostles, who prayed and laid their hands on them.

— Acts 6:1–6

Speak out for those who cannot speak, for the rights of all the destitute. Speak out, judge righteously, defend the rights of the poor and needy.

— Proverbs 31:8–9

Do not make fun of one who is ill-bred, or your ancestors may be insulted.

— Ecclesiasticus 8:4

{ CHAPTER 12 }

Assessing Resources

A Story

Dulce left Mexico when she was 16. She had completed the third grade in her native country and knew no English. In her mid-20s she found herself in Houston, a single mom with three small girls and expecting a fourth. She had few friends, no way to hold a job, still no English, and basically little hope of escaping from the situation that held her and her children.

She met two Christian women who took an interest in her family, and together they started on a path that changed all their lives. The story of Dulce and her girls might make a good book, and she's thinking about writing it, too. They were embraced by a Christian congregation. Many different people took their part in many different ways: food, clothing, emotional support, training in parenting and life, heart surgery for the youngest girl, and guidance through the bureaucratic mazes that make up life in the city. Dulce learned English, got help with the girls, began work, bought a car, obtained U.S. citizenship, and was granted the opportunity to work for and move into a Habitat for Humanity house. All the while she struggled with all the battles any other mother would face with four daughters.

The girls are now women. There are two sons-in-law and two grandchildren. Dulce cleans houses and offices for a positive living. She faces the future with many friends, a faith that God will care for her and enough resources to be a help to others as she was once helped.

How did it happen? There was the constant help of dozens of men and women and the occasional support of a hundred more . . . One more thing: 28 years have passed.

Jesus told his disciples to count the cost. He meant the cost of discipleship. Many Christians through the ages have sought to keep the cost as low as possible, sometimes hoping for a free ride. The gifted Christian who offers little to the poor in the community may well have lost sight of his/her true task and calling as a Christian. "Sight" is the operative word here. Can we "see" the path ahead as we embrace the poor? Probably not clearly, but we may find footing for the next step.

EVALUATING THE SITUATION

Those who have attempted to help even a single stranger know that you may start and even finish one situation, but you invariably uncover more needs. The story of the Jerusalem church in Acts 6 illustrates the point. At first glance the story seems to speak against the apostles: They were handing off the poor folks to others. Considering the situation more closely, however, brings an entirely different understanding. The church at that time exceeded 5,000 believers (Acts 4:4). In that kind of group, we could guess there were 500 widows. Each of the seven new deacons might have been moving around more than a half-ton of food every week. They would have been busy people. There would be the gathering of the food, some storage, the organizing of its distribution, some clerical work (the initial problem was that some widows had been left out), and the inevitable encountering of other needs as the food was delivered. Attempts to help others can take on rapidly expanding dimensions. The apostles intended to continue their first charge of preaching and teaching. They also could see physical needs that required attention. They were able to continue their work by calling out and placing the deacons over the tasks that needed doing. Today, in our ministries with the poor, we would do well to learn from the example of the early church—and to make a reasonable assessment of the size of the tasks at hand.

RESOURCES INVENTORY

The Resources Inventory was developed to help quantify resources in order to better plan where to expend time, money, and energy.

The eight life resources described in Chapter 8 serve as the basis for the Resources Inventory (below). This tool can give a fairly clear sense of an individual's strength or need relative to others. From 0 to 3 points are given in each of the resource areas (financial, emotional, mental, etc.), giving a potential total score of up to 24 for all eight. The meanings of the total scores are discussed on the following pages.

Resources Inventory
Score 1 point for each box checked.

FINANCIAL
- ❑ Enough food; living under a roof
- ❑ Positive direction; paying bills
- ❑ Extras, including some luxuries

EMOTIONAL
- ❑ Not violent, verbally or physically
- ❑ Functioning under normal stress; can consider choices
- ❑ Emotional support for self and others

MENTAL
- ❑ Able to learn; can read
- ❑ High school diploma or base skills
- ❑ College or special training

SPIRITUAL
- ❑ Not feeling hopeless
- ❑ Has spiritual roots
- ❑ Has spiritual strength; can guide others

PHYSICAL
- ❑ Not sick; can care for self in own home
- ❑ Healthy; can go to work and travel about freely
- ❑ Strong /attractive

SUPPORT SYSTEMS
- ❑ Help from family
- ❑ Help from friends
- ❑ Help from powerful friends

ROLE MODELS
- ❑ Not negative
- ❑ Positive
- ❑ Positive in one's own field

KNOWLEDGE OF HIDDEN RULES
- ❑ Understands own group
- ❑ Understands second group
- ❑ Understands third group

HOW TO USE THE INVENTORY

■ Choose two individuals to score — one from a poor economic setting, the other from wealth. Place their initials at the top of two of the columns on the Resources Scoring Chart below. At first, you might try two well-developed fictional characters like Huck Finn and Bruce Wayne/Batman.

■ Score each of the individuals on each resource on the Resources Scoring Chart from 0 to 3 points, according to the criteria in the Resources Inventory.

■ Add the scores for each in the TOTAL row.

Resources Scoring Chart

RESOURCES	INITIALS					
Financial						
Emotional						
Mental						
Spiritual						
Physical						
Support systems						
Role models						
Knowledge of hidden rules						
TOTAL						
Liabilities						
Momentum						

INDIVIDUAL SCORES IN RESOURCE AREAS

Financial: Score the individuals 1 point if they have food and shelter (even from someone else); 2 points if their income or finances are such that they are paying their bills and eating regularly; or 3 points if they can afford expensive cars, homes, and entertainments.

Emotional: Scoring begins with 1 point if they are not violent or emotionally shut down. Give 2 points if they can make decisions under normal stress at work and home. Three points are for those who can offer emotional support to others.

Mental: Give 1 point if they can learn (usually meaning "can read"); 2 points for high school diploma or a viable trade skill; and 3 points for college or specialty training.

Spiritual: Give 1 point if they wake up most days with a sense of positive possibilities for the day; 2 points if they have spiritual roots from their family (a sense of a loving God and moral guidance); 3 points if their spiritual strength can help guide others.

Physical: If they aren't sick this week (moving around on their own and caring for themselves), they get 1 point; 2 points if they're healthy (out and about); and 3 points if they're strong and/or attractive.

Support systems: In this area individuals get 1 point each for friends and family support (if they have both, they get 2 points). Having powerful friends (community or church leaders, people who can influence others or get things done) would score 1 more point.

Role models: If they don't function with negative role models, they get 1 point; 2 points if they have positive models; and 3 if their role models are positive and doing what they are doing. (For example, a young teacher with a positive role model who is also a teacher has advantages over the young teacher whose positive model is an engineer.)

Knowledge of hidden rules: If they understand the rules of their current subculture they get 1 point. (An adolescent might attend but not yet understand high school. A recent immigrant might not understand his/her new country.) They get 2 points if they understand a second culture or economic group. (A woman who cleans houses may live in poverty, but she may come to understand higher economic groups.) They get 3 points if they understand three groups. (A successful restaurant manager will need to deal with affluent customers, vendors, delivery drivers, the wait staff, and the newest busboy. A church leader must understand at least the economic group that makes up the congregation where he/she serves. It would be better to know even more.)

Liabilities: Mark the number of dependents the person already cares for, or give some sort of estimate of the number of persons dependent on them. A parent with four children who shares duties evenly with his/her spouse could be charged with two of those children fully. A partly disabled parent in the individual's home might add another ½. Other people they already help should be considered and added accordingly.

Momentum: In this box give some sense of the individual's progress or decline. A normal child can fairly be expected to grow in his/her score. A senior individual might be declining in physical or other resources. Many adults can be expected to operate for years on a single level. Mark the box with an arrow pointing up, down, or level (pointing both directions).

Before reading further, you might want to score a few more individuals. Consider individuals you know well: infants, teens, adults in various situations, powerful adults, residents in nursing homes, et al.

Meaning of Scores: the Numbers

The chart below gives some sense of the meaning of the number scores.

Generally, this is what is found. The higher the score, the more the individual will be able to help others and the less he/she will need help. The lower the score, the more the individual will need assistance and the less he/she will be able to help. Every congregation is a mix of higher- and lower-scoring individuals. Regarding resources, the goal of a church is not to have as few low scores as possible, tempting as that might be. Rather, it is to effectively connect people who do not have many resources with those who do.

Scores of more than 16 indicate those who are able to give more than they receive. Gifted teenagers or young adults might score a 17. Such teens might well be leaders among their peers and already full of promise in their next steps in life. A score of 20 or above is usually from adults of potential or actual position among their peers. Such individuals are in a position to offer strength to others. Within a church, the high scorers should not be the target of many programs to help and guide people. They are the ones who ought to do the helping and guiding.

A disclaimer before going farther: The Resources Inventory is a tool to quantify the resources individuals have for bearing their own and others' burdens. Scores on the Resources Inventory are not an indicator of anyone's standing with God or with his/her church.

Regarding an individual's score under "spiritual" resources, fluctuations from 0 to 3 can be found in the normal course of life. To become a Christian is to confess the need for the grace of God through Christ, hardly a claim of spiritual strength. And even the strongest spiritual leaders can have low times. Their standing with God is not necessarily thereby affected.

Similarly, total scores, low or high, are not direct indicators of someone's standing in his/her congregation. We have all known people on their death-bed who still wielded considerable positive influence even as they required constant physical help. Conversely, you have Biblical examples like Pharaoh, Herod, and even the Christian-persecuting Pharisee, Saul of Tarsus—all heavily resourced but hardly in good standing with God's people. The bishops and deacons described in 1 Timothy 3 would be high-scoring individuals. Any church would be blessed to have a house full of them, but where would a shepherd be without some sheep? A healthy congregation is a mixture of those who are serving and those being served, with few among them doing only one or the other.

Generally, those scoring below 16 receive more than they give. Those scoring 13 to 15 might be teens who are still dependent on their parents or others. They also might be adults in some difficulty. In either case, if they are regularly around a church, that church will be expending resources of time, money, and energy on them. Adults who score in this range and below sometimes receive a fairly tepid welcome when they first present themselves to a congregation. This is understandable, as most churches hope for people who can be contributing additions to the flock. At the least they might hope for members who will not be too much of a drain. Families and individuals can be passively (or even passively/aggressively) repulsed by a church that does not expend resources on them.

Scores below 14 indicate greater need for care. Those below 9 are usually infants, children, or adults in need of daily attention or assistance.

A low score does not mean individuals cannot help others. Rather, it means they will likely be receiving plenty of help themselves. Teens can be of great service in many settings, but they also need training and supervision that require expenditure of resources. In the case of teens, the hope is for greater returns in the future from those being assisted now.

Conversely, it should be noted that a high score does not necessarily indicate where someone is spending his/her resources. Greatly gifted individuals may choose to spend their resources on themselves and their family.

Meaning of Scores: Time

A given score represents only a moment in time. Scores will change during an individual's life as the years pass. A child grows up. Adults may lose their health. Individuals who have low resources today may have higher ones tomorrow. Dulce, in the story at the beginning of this chapter, scored no higher than a 12 when she was first contacted. She now scores no lower than an 18. For an exercise showing this, someone who is theologically inclined might score David of the Old Testament in three stages of his life: as a young shepherd standing before Goliath, as a king in his prime before he saw Bathsheba, and as an old man of failing health before he gives the crown to Solomon.

This book is designed to help church members help others. Ideally, this will mean that many of those who are helped will become great helpers and servants themselves.

Meaning of Scores: Liabilities and Momentum

The two rows at the bottom of the Resources Scoring Chart on page 112 help round out the picture for a given individual. Neither of these items changes an individual's score, but they do help provide a clearer picture of the individual's needs and his/her ability to help others now and in the future.

Liabilities: Everyone who has resources can take on burdens, but there will be a limit to what they can do. A single youth scoring 16 might well have more to offer in time and effort than a young parent who has two infants to raise. Just because individuals have a high score does not mean they are unencumbered. A high-scoring church leader might be able to take on one family in need or even two, but this will affect the time and energy left for other projects.

The situation becomes more critical for the person who has a low score. A single mother with few resources may use virtually all of them caring for her children. Whether an individual's score is low or high, his/her ability to help the next person is adversely affected by how many people he/she already is helping.

Momentum: Individuals go through transitions in life. Such transitions can set the stage for the next days or years. We expect children to grow into adults. They may score low today, but have the promise of higher scores. Their momentum is positive. In life there are also plateaus, and scores can stay level for long periods. At other times the resources of life may wane, even spiral down. Many times a church will encounter a family only when it is spiraling downward.

WHERE TO BEGIN

When individuals or churches commit to helping people (see Acts 6 on page 108), they will do well to assess their situation and the particulars of those they would serve.

Study Your Community

There are plenty of good sources for facts about your community. Local schools and school districts are often required to keep precise demographic and economic data. As this information is accessible, it is very useful.

The U.S. Bureau of the Census offers a mountain of data specific to individual counties and many cities. The current Internet address is www.census.gov. To gain a clear picture, look at your county and the counties that surround it. Go there; take notes. You'll be glad you did.

Study Your Resources

The Resources Inventory will help you and your congregation have a sense of what you have to share and the limits of your resources. Spiritual resources are, of course, the bread and butter of a church, but these tend to develop slowly within the individual. The same could be said of emotional and mental resources. Role models take some time too, but they begin to emerge when contact occurs between people. After financial resources, support systems have the most direct application for a church. Transportation, childcare, help with financial and insurance problems, directions to better business and service companies . . . all can have significant impact while spending relatively little money.

The distribution of financial resources presents certain complications. On the one hand, those who help at all will sometimes be helping with money. (Consider question 1 at the end of this chapter.) On the other hand, this should be done with care. Generally, cash should not be given to the person in need, but directly to the vendor, doctor, utility. In the long run, the greater good usually arrives through the other resources.

Be creative! In your regular congregational gatherings, try to include some mundane information about hidden rules (attire, basic courtesies, language, etc.) or other wisdom directly related to daily life and needs. You also might design other gatherings specifically planned to teach basic life skills about money, food, transportation, communication, education, and more. Train your church members how to become advocates for those in need. For example, one of the most effective tools for the helper, male or female, is a moderately conservative business suit. It is impressive how well doctors, lawyers, judges, police officers, educators, and assorted bureaucrats behave when an otherwise resourceless person arrives escorted by someone in a suit!

By all means, recognize the hidden rules of your own culture and church.

Study Those You're Aiming to Serve

Individual conversations (just working together may do) will present a clearer picture of needs and sensitive areas of the people you serve. When you see patterns of need, consider those needs first. Always realize that as you cross cultural chasms, you risk breeches of etiquette; however, doors likely will open to all sorts of communication once you learn the hidden rules of poverty. At the very least, most folks will appreciate that you're trying to tune in to their lives.

Keep your eyes and ears open to surprises from those you help. As individuals arrive in our midst from other economic and ethnic cultures, they bring useful gifts and skills. There is nothing really new here. The advantage is to those who watch for the unexpected. Middle- and upper-class cultures solve problems in their own ways, ways generally known within those cultures. Lower economic cultures solve problems too. I have watched in awe as conflict was resolved by individuals who have never operated from a position of power. The abilities and talents of those you help might be yours as well, if you bother to notice them; indeed, the help could soon be flowing both ways.

Count the Cost

Helping others will take money, time, energy, and emotion. There will be limits to what can be done by any individual or congregation. Not long after developing the Resources Inventory, I began to wonder how an inner-city congregation might manage the burden of its efforts. One such congregation that serves a mostly poor membership offered this assessment of its annual investment: 38 years' worth of work (salaried and volunteer), based on 40 hours a week for 52 weeks, for a membership of about 900. A more middle-class congregation served its membership of 400 in only six such years.

Specialize

Knowing that the poor will always be with us (as Jesus himself said), we might despair. We would be better served to specialize. Pick one niche that suits your gifts and start there. It may be as much as you can do for a while. It likely will be appreciated, if only minimally (remember, only one of the 10 lepers thanked Jesus). If done well, it will become known. Other needs will be presented. When you're ready, you might expand. One thing is fairly certain: You will be learning all along the way.

QUESTIONS

1. Read Luke 10:29–37 (the Good Samaritan). How does the Samaritan score on the Resources Inventory? Do you know Christians who could have done all the things he did? Describe them. What could a less-resourced Christian do for the man?

2. Get the "QuickFacts" for your county from the U.S. Bureau of the Census. What things stand out to you?

3. What are the strengths of the members of your congregation?

4. In the short run, what could your church offer to people in need?
    In the long run?

5. Have you ever noticed something wise or useful in another culture?
    If so, what application could it have to your culture and congrega-
    tion?

SCRIPTURES

If then there is any encouragement in Christ, any consolation from love, any sharing in the Spirit, any compassion and sympathy, make my joy complete: be of the same mind, having the same love, being in full accord and of one mind. Do nothing from selfish ambition or conceit, but in humility regard others as better than yourselves. Let each of you look not to your own interests, but to the interests of others. Let the same mind be in you that was in Christ Jesus, who, though he was in the form of God, did not regard equality with God as something to be exploited, but emptied himself, taking the form of a slave, being born in human likeness. And being found in human form, he humbled himself and became obedient to the point of death— even death on a cross.

– Philippians 2:1–8

I appeal to you therefore, brothers and sisters, by the mercies of God, to present your bodies as a living sacrifice, holy and acceptable to God, which is your spiritual worship. Do not be conformed to this world, but be transformed by the renewing of your minds, so that you may discern what is the will of God—what is good and acceptable and perfect. For by the grace given to me I say to everyone among you not to think of yourself more highly than you ought to think, but to think with sober judgment, each according to the measure of faith that God has assigned. For as in one body we have many members, and not all the members have the same function, so we, who are many, are one body in Christ, and individually we are members one of another. We have gifts that differ according to the grace given to us: prophecy, in proportion to faith; ministry, in ministering; the teacher, in teaching; the exhorter, in exhortation; the giver, in generosity; the leader, in diligence; the compassionate, in cheerfulness. Let love be genuine; hate what is evil, hold fast to what is good; love one another with mutual affection; outdo one another in showing honor. Do not lag in zeal, be ardent in spirit, serve the Lord. Rejoice in hope, be patient in suffering, persevere in prayer. Contribute to the needs of the saints; extend hospitality to strangers. Bless those who persecute you; bless and do not curse them. Rejoice with those who rejoice, weep with those who weep. Live in harmony with one another; do not be haughty, but associate with the lowly; do not claim to be wiser than you are. Do not repay anyone evil for evil, but take thought for what is noble in the sight of all. If it is possible, so far as it depends on you, live peaceably with all. Beloved, never avenge yourselves, but leave room for the wrath of God; for it is written, "Vengeance is mine, I will repay, says the Lord." No, "if your enemies are hungry, feed them; if they are thirsty, give them something to drink; for by doing this you will heap burning coals on their heads." Do not be overcome by evil, but overcome evil with good.

– Romans 12:1–21

CHAPTER 13

Conclusion

A Story

It was a big church. The members included many who were leaders in the community. Also there were many families who had been significant in not only the congregation's own growth but also in the building of churches all around. Many were proud of their congregation—that it was strong, that it was important to the lives of many, that it held up the truth of the Gospel to the world.

Their preacher was a gifted speaker and one whose heart was clearly loving and open to even the most difficult problems facing them all. He had great affection for not only that congregation but also the whole fellowship of which they were a part. One Sunday he spoke from his heart about a dilemma he felt with great sorrow. With candor he asked the question, "Why are we here?" and related some of his greater fears. Were they there because that was just their family's tradition? Was it just good business to be part of that great congregation? Was their connection only to last until something better came along? Christianity was supposed to spring from a deep conviction of spiritual need and a face-to-face connection with a just and loving God. Had they bypassed a true conversion for a cheap faith, which offered only comfort to those already comfortable? Were they no more than a big, proud club?

The sermon was heard in stunned silence. It was clear. It was honest. It asked questions that few had had the nerve to express. The message pierced the congregation's very soul . . . The next week the church's leaders fired the preacher.

Almost immediately, they reconsidered and asked the preacher to stay. He did and served there more than another decade. Still, 25 years later, the sermon remains notorious and a matter of great sensitivity.

Not everyone wants to be "saved." One of the myths of middle class is that everyone wants to be middle class. *Not true.* There are some freedoms in poverty that simply are not found in middle class—freedom of speech, freedom of relationships, freedom of behavior. Yet often these unrestricted freedoms cause much pain and heartbreak for those in generational poverty. So the key issue is this: Have we provided the support, teaching, and relationships that will allow these persons to move into a more stable, constructive, and spiritual life *if they so desire*?

Churches tend to make the greatest inroads with children and their mothers. In the research, mothers are key determiners of the level of education the children receive. Educational attainment is a direct correlate of whether a person lives in poverty or not. So involvement with mothers and their children is critical to turning the pattern around.

But in serving the poor, one also must learn to grieve.

One of the topics as yet untouched is the need to grieve and go through the grieving process as one ministers to, teaches, or works with the poor. The Kübler-Ross stages in the grieving process are anger, denial, bargaining, depression, and acceptance. As one meets and works with a particular family or individual, there is much frustration and ultimately, grieving, because many situations are so embedded as to seem hopeless. It is like dealing with the legendary octopus; each time a tentacle is removed, another appears. Particularly for the adults, so many choices have been made that virtually preclude any resolution that would be acceptable from an educated perspective. Yet the role of the educator, social worker, employer, or church worker is not necessarily to save the individual but rather to offer a support system, role models, and opportunities to learn, which will increase the likelihood of the person's success. Ultimately, the choice always belongs to the individual.

Yet another notion among the middle class and educated is that if the poor had a choice, they would live differently. The financial resources would certainly help make a difference. Even with the financial resources, however, not every individual who received that money would choose to live differently. As alluded to above, there is a freedom of verbal expression; an appreciation of individual personality; a heightened and intense emotional experience; and a sensual, kinesthetic approach to life usually not found in the middle class or among the educated. These characteristics are so ingrained into the daily life of the poor that to have those cut off would be to lose a limb. Many choose not to live a different life. And for some individuals, alcoholism, laziness, lack of motivation, drug addiction, etc., make the choices, in effect, *for* them.

But it's the responsibility of church workers and others who work with the poor to teach the differences and skills/rules that will allow the individual to make the choice. As it now stands for many of the poor, that choice never exists.

QUESTIONS

1. What skills do you need to better understand the poor? Where could you get these skills?

2. Consider the members who comprise your congregation's financial base. How open are they to the inclusion of different cultural and economic groups?

3. It's easy to be right and still greatly offend people. The valuable skill is to be able to share life-changing facts in a way that will be heard and considered. How can we bring along individuals whose ideas of Christianity were formed in a very different world?

{ APPENDIX }

Statistical Charts on Poverty

The following pages present data published in 2004 by the U.S. Bureau of the Census, which publishes income and poverty charts each fall for the previous calendar year. For the most current information provided in this format, visit www.ahaprocess.com.

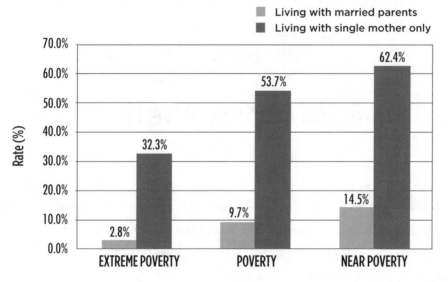

Extreme Poverty, Poverty, and Near-Poverty Rates for Children Under 5 by Living Arrangement: 2003

Living with married parents
Living with single mother only

Source: U.S. Bureau of the Census

Household Income in 20% Increments of Total: 2003

Group	Average Household Income Ranges: 2003
LOWEST 20%	$0 – $17,984
SECOND 20%	$17,985 – $34,000
THIRD 20%	$34,001 – $54,440
FOURTH 20%	$54,441 – $86,860
HIGHEST 20%	$86,861+
TOP 5% (part of highest 20%)	$154,120+

Source: U.S. Bureau of the Census

U.S. Median Income for Persons Age 25 and Older, by Sex and Educational Attainment: 2003

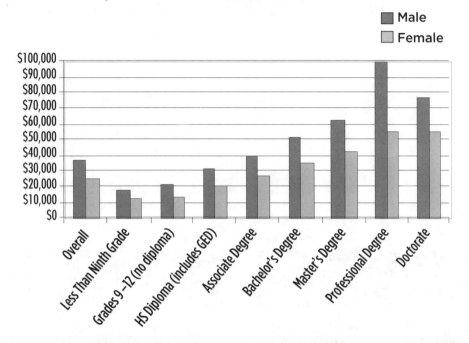

Educational attainment	Number of persons (in thousands) with income		Median income in 2003 dollars	
	Male	Female	Male	Female
Overall	89,558	97,319	$37,288	$25,499
Less Than Ninth Grade	5,804	5,943	$18,710	$12,978
Grades 9–12 (no diploma)	7,766	8,233	$22,196	$13,695
HS Diploma (includes GED)	27,889	31,921	$31,411	$20,759
Associate Degree	6,751	9,013	$40,454	$26,872
Bachelor's Degree	16,632	17,134	$51,507	$35,109
Master's Degree	6,157	6,451	$62,495	$42,466
Professional Degree	1,925	1,027	$100,000	$56,143
Doctorate	1,621	801	$77,525	$56,182

Source: U.S. Bureau of the Census

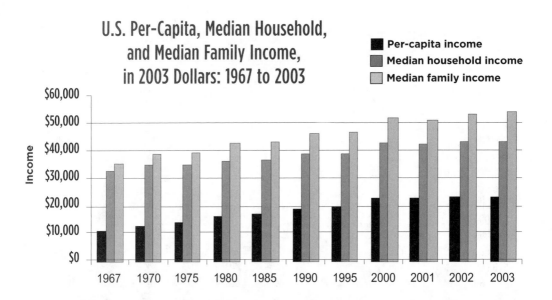

U.S. Per-Capita, Median Household, and Median Family Income, in 2003 Dollars: 1967 to 2003

Year	Per-Capita Income	Median Household Income	Median Family Income
2003	$23,276	$43,318	$53,991
2002	23,318	43,381	53,911
2001	22,851	42,228	51,407
2000	22,970	43,162	52,148
1999	22,499	43,355	51,996
1998	21,821	42,173	50,689
1997	21,162	40,699	49,017
1996	20,372	39,869	47,516
1995	19,871	39,306	46,843
1994	19,559	38,119	45,820
1993	19,033	37,688	44,586
1992	18,358	37,880	45,221
1991	18,526	38,183	45,551
1990	18,894	39,324	46,429
1989	19,378	38,850	47,166
1988	18,868	39,144	46,285
1987	18,465	38,835	46,151
1986	17,983	38,365	45,393
1985	17,280	37,059	43,518

Year	Per-Capita Income	Median Household Income	Median Family Income
1984	16,476	36,343	42,858
1983	16,008	35,214	41,444
1982	15,770	35,423	41,151
1981	15,766	35,478	41,652
1980	15,844	36,035	42,776
1979	16,196	37,059	44,255
1978	15,955	37,180	43,601
1977	14,914	35,777	41,271
1976	14,456	35,581	41,023
1975	13,972	34,980	39,784
1974	13,958	35,943	40,513
1973	14,291	37,104	41,590
1972	13,821	36,386	40,764
1971	12,916	34,897	38,787
1970	12,543	35,232	39,954
1969	12,443	35,472	39,034
1968	11,793	34,217	37,275
1967	11,067	32,783	35,629

Source: U.S. Bureau of the Census

Percentage of U.S. Persons Below Poverty Level, by Race and Ethnicity: 1976 to 2003

- ◆ Total
- ■ Black
- ⊠ White
- ▲ Hispanic

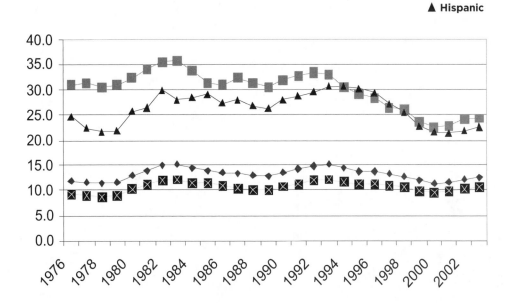

Year	Total	Black	White	Hispanic
2003	12.5	24.4	10.5	22.5
2002	12.1	24.1	10.2	21.8
2001	11.7	22.7	9.9	21.4
2000	11.3	22.5	9.5	21.5
1999	11.9	23.6	9.8	22.7
1998	12.7	26.1	10.5	25.6
1997	13.3	26.5	11.0	27.1
1996	13.7	28.4	11.2	29.4
1995	13.8	29.3	11.2	30.3
1994	14.5	30.6	11.7	30.7
1993	15.1	33.1	12.2	30.6
1992	14.8	33.4	11.9	29.6
1991	14.2	32.7	11.3	28.7
1990	13.5	31.9	10.7	28.1

Year	Total	Black	White	Hispanic
1989	12.8	30.7	10.0	26.2
1988	13.0	31.3	10.1	26.7
1987	13.4	32.4	10.4	28.0
1986	13.6	31.1	11.0	27.3
1985	14.0	31.3	11.4	29.0
1984	14.4	33.8	11.5	28.4
1983	15.2	35.7	12.1	28.0
1982	15.0	35.6	12.0	29.9
1981	14.0	34.2	11.1	26.5
1980	13.0	32.5	10.2	25.7
1979	11.7	31.0	9.0	21.8
1978	11.4	30.6	8.7	21.6
1977	11.6	31.3	8.9	22.4
1976	11.8	31.1	9.1	24.7

Source: U.S. Bureau of the Census

BIBLIOGRAPHY

Bianchi, Suzanne M. (1990). America's Children: Mixed Prospects. *Population Bulletin.* Volume 45. Number 1. June.

Boals, Beverly M., et al. (1990). *Children in Poverty: Providing and Promoting a Quality Education.* Education Research Information Consortium document.

Bradshaw, John. (1988). *Bradshaw on: The Family.* Deerfield Beach, FL: Health Communications.

Capponi, Pat. (1997). *Dispatches from the Poverty Line.* Toronto, Ontario, Canada: Penguin Books.

Collins, Bryn C. (1997). *Emotional Unavailability: Recognizing It, Understanding It, and Avoiding Its Trap.* Lincolnwood, IL: NTC/Contemporary Publishing Company.

Comer, James. (1995). Lecture given at Education Service Center, Region IV. Houston, TX.

Cook, John T., & Brown, Larry J. (1993). *Two Americas: Racial Differences in Child Poverty in the U.S.: A Linear Trend Analysis to the Year 2010.* Research-in-progress working paper. Medford, MA: Tufts University.

Coontz, Stephanie. (1995). The American Family and the Nostalgia Trap. *Phi Delta Kappan.* Volume 76. Number 7. March.

Covey, Stephen R. (1989). *The Seven Habits of Highly Effective People: Powerful Lessons in Personal Change.* New York, NY: Simon & Schuster.

Duncan, Greg J., & Brooks-Gunn, Jeanne. (Eds.). (1997). *Consequences of Growing Up Poor.* New York, NY: Russell Sage Foundation.

Edelman, Peter B., & Ladner, Joyce. (Eds.). (1991). *Adolescence and Poverty: Challenge for the 1990's.* Washington, DC: Center for National Policy.

Five Million Children: 1992 Update. (1992). New York, NY: National Center for Children in Poverty, Columbia University.

Forward, Susan, with Frazier, Donna. (n.d.). *Emotional Blackmail.* New York, NY: HarperCollins Publishers.

Fussel, Paul. (1983). *Class.* New York, NY: Ballantine Books.

Garmezy, Norman. (1991). Resiliency and Vulnerability to Adverse Developmental Outcomes Associated with Poverty. *American Behavioral Scientist.* Volume 34. Number 4. March–April. pp. 416–430.

Goleman, Daniel. (1995). *Emotional Intelligence.* New York, NY: Bantam Books.

Harrington, Michael. (1962). *The Other America.* New York, NY: Simon & Schuster.

Joos, Martin. (1967). The Styles of the Five Clocks. *Language and Cultural Diversity in American Education.* 1972. Abrahams, R.D., & Troike, R.C. (Eds.). Englewood Cliffs, NJ: Prentice-Hall.

Kozol, Jonathan. (1991). *Savage Inequalities.* New York, NY: HarperPerennial.

Kozol, Jonathan. (1995). *Amazing Grace.* New York, NY: Crown Publishers.

Laborde, Genie Z. (1983). *Influencing with Integrity: Management Skills for Communication and Negotiation.* Palo Alto, CA: Syntony Publishing.

Language Barriers Are More Complex Than We Might Think. (1992). *CSBA News.* Sacramento, CA: California School Boards Association. Volume 4. Number 9. November.

Larson, Jackie. (1993). Maria Montano-Harmon: A Call for Heightened Awareness. *Texas Lone Star.* November.

Lewis, Anne C. (1996). Breaking the Cycle of Poverty. *Phi Delta Kappan.* Volume 78. Number 3. November.

Lewit, Eugene M. (1993). Child Indicators: Children in Poverty. *Future-of-Children.* Volume 3. Number 1. Spring.

Lewit, Eugene M. (1993). Why Is Poverty Increasing Among Children? *Future-of-Children.* Volume 3. Number 2. Summer/Fall.

Mayer, Susan E. (1997). *What Money Can't Buy.* Cambridge, MA: Harvard University Press.

Mills, C. Wright. (1956). *The Power Elite.* New York, NY: Oxford University Press.

Miranda, Leticia C. (1991). *Latino Child Poverty in the United States.* Washington, DC: Children's Defense Fund.

Montano-Harmon, Maria Rosario. (1991). Discourse Features of Written Mexican Spanish: Current Research in Contrastive Rhetoric and Its Implications. *Hispania.* Volume 74. Number 2. May. pp. 417–425.

New Revised Standard Version Bible. (1989). Division of Christian Eudcation of the National Council of the Churches of Christ in the USA. Grand Rapids, MI: Zondervan Bible Publishers.

Penchef, Esther. (Ed.). (1971). *Four Horsemen: Pollution, Poverty, Famine, Violence.* San Francisco, CA: Canfield Press.

Renchler, Ron. (1993). Poverty and Learning. *ERIC Digest.* Number 83. Eugene, OR: Education Research Information Consortium Clearinghouse on Educational Management.

Rodriguez, Luis J. (1993). *Always Running.* New York, NY: Simon & Schuster.

Samuelson, Robert J. (1997). The Culture of Poverty. *Newsweek.* Volume 129. Number 18. May 5.

Sennett, Richard, & Cobb, Jonathan. (1993). *The Hidden Injuries of Class.* London/Boston: Faber & Faber. First published in USA in 1972 by Alfred A. Knopf, New York, NY.

Shapiro, Joseph P., Friedman, Dorian, Meyer, Michelle, & Loftus, Margaret. (1996). Invincible Kids. *U.S. News & World Report.* Volume 121. Number 19. November 11.

Sharron, Howard, & Coulter, Martha. (1994). *Changing Children's Minds: Feuerstein's Revolution in the Teaching of Intelligence.* Exeter, Great Britain: BPC Wheatons Ltd.

Stern, Mark J. (1987). The Welfare of Families. *Educational Leadership.* March. pp. 82–87.

Takeuchi, David T., et al. (1991). Economic Stress in the Family and Children's Emotional and Behavioral Problems. *Journal of Marriage and the Family.* Volume 53. Number 4. November. pp. 1031–1041.

The Poorest Among Us. (1996). *U.S. News & World Report.* Volume 121. Number 25. December 23.

Vobejda, Barbara. (1994). Half of Nation's Kids Not in "Typical" Family. *Houston Chronicle.* August 30.

Wake Up America: Columbia University Study Shatters Stereotypes of Young Child Poverty. (1996). Internet Website: http://cpmcnet.columbia.edu/news/press_releases/12-11-96.html. December 11.

Wheatley, Margaret J. (1992). *Leadership and the New Science.* San Francisco, CA: Berrett-Koehler Publishers.

Zill, Nicholaus. (1993). The Changing Realities of Family Life. *Aspen Institute Quarterly.* Volume 5. Number 1. Winter. pp. 27–51.

ABOUT THE AUTHORS

Ruby K. Payne, Ph.D., of Baytown, Texas, has been a professional educator since 1972, serving as a secondary teacher and department chairperson, elementary principal, and central-office administrator.

Since 1994 Dr. Payne, founder and president of aha! Process, Inc., has been sharing her insights about the culture of poverty—and how to help educators and other professionals work effectively with children and adults from that culture—in more than a thousand workshop settings throughout North America, Australia, and India.

Since publishing her seminal work, *A Framework for Understanding Poverty* in 1995, Dr. Payne also has written or co-authored nearly a dozen books surrounding these issues in such areas as education, social services, the workplace, faith communities, and leadership.

She received her B.A. from Goshen (IN) College. She earned a master's degree from Western Michigan University and her doctorate from Loyola (IL) University.

Bill Ehlig has been a minister at the Missouri Street Church of Christ in Baytown, Texas, since 1980. It was in this same community that he lived the second half of his childhood. The community has gone through some of the same phases that have changed and troubled many of the oil-based economies of Texas and Louisiana.

Ehlig received his training for ministry at Abilene Christian University. His master's degree is in Ancient Church History. He also has worked with churches in Scotland, Romania, and Mexico.

He enjoys spending time with his wife, Margaret, and their three children, Alison, Eric, and Kirk. He is interested in birds and nature studies and in figuring out just how a 2,000-year-old church can address these amazing times.

Eye-openers at ...
www.ahaprocess.com

- If you are interested in more information regarding seminars or training for *A Framework for Understanding Poverty* or other offerings, we invite you to visit our Website, www.ahaprocess.com.

- There you also can join our *aha!* News List. Receive the latest income and poverty statistics *free* when you join! Then periodic news and updates will follow.

- If you would like to read the latest articles written by Dr. Ruby K. Payne, look for the link on our Website homepage.

- Additional programs/video series offered by aha! Process, Inc. include:
    Sermons on audio to accompany this book
    Preventing School Violence by Creating Emotional Safety
    Meeting Standards & Raising Test Scores—When You Don't Have Much Time or Money
    Bridges Out of Poverty: Strategies for Professionals and Communities
    Removing the Mask: Giftedness in Poverty
    Tucker Signing Strategies for Reading
    Learning Structures

- For a complete listing of products, please visit www.ahaprocess.com.

{ ORDER FORM }

Want your own copies? Want to give a copy to a friend?

Please send me _____ copy/copies of *What Every Church Member Should Know About Poverty.* Enclosed is payment for:

Books $ _____

Shipping $ _____

Subtotal $ _____

Sales tax $ _____
(6.25%, Texas residents only)

Total $ _____

1–4 BOOKS:
$22.00/each + $4.50 first book, plus
        $2.00 each additional book,
        shipping/handling

5 OR MORE BOOKS:
$15.00/each + 8% shipping/handling

UPS Ship-to Address (no post office boxes, please)

Name_____

Organization _____

Address _____

_____

Phone _____

E-mail _____

Method of Payment

Purchase order # _____

Credit card type_____   Exp. _____

Credit card # _____

Check $ _____   Check # _____

Thanks for your order!

www.ahaprocess.com

PO Box 727 • Highlands, TX 77562-0727
(800) 424-9484 • fax (281) 426-5600